ALMONDS

ALMONDS

Recipes, History, Culture

BARBARA BRYANT AND BETSY FENTRESS

RECIPES BY LYNDA BALSLEV
WITH CONTRIBUTIONS FROM CELEBRATED CHEFS AND FOOD WRITERS
PHOTOGRAPHS BY ROBERT HOLMES

GIBBS SMITH
TO ENRICH AND INSPIRE HUMANKIND

First Edition
18 17 16 15 14   5 4 3 2 1

Text © 2014 Watermark Publishing, LLC
Photographs © 2014 Robert Holmes Photography
Photographs © 2014 Andrea Johnson, pages 49, 59, 130, 143
Additional image credits on page 157
Recipes by Lynda Balslev; recipes on pages 74, 124, and 143
    contributed by Barbara Bryant

Published by
Gibbs Smith
P.O. Box 667
Layton, Utah 84041

1.800.835.4993 orders
www.gibbs-smith.com

Designed and produced by Jennifer Barry Design, Fairfax, California
Food styling by Kim Kissling
Edited by Barbara Bryant and Betsy Fentress
Printed and bound in China

Library of Congress Cataloging-in-Publication Data

Bryant, Barbara, 1947-
  Almonds : recipes, history, culture / Barbara Bryant and Betsy
Fentress ; recipes by Lynda Balslev ; with contributions from
celebrated chefs and food writers ; photographs by Robert Holmes.
— First edition.
    pages cm
  Includes index.
  ISBN 978-1-4236-3464-5
  1. Cooking (Almonds) I. Fentress, Betsy. II. Balslev, Lynda. III. Title.
TX814.2.A44B79 2014
641.6'455—dc23
                              2013027161

CONTENTS

Preface

When did I first fall in love with almonds? As a child, I remember walking to the Village Store in St. Louis with my monthly allowance of 25 cents. It was a tiny spot, with a lovely section of candy at my eye level. The woman behind the counter would hand us a small brown bag, into which we would place our carefully chosen treasures: jawbreakers, gum balls, wax lips, Lik-M-Aid, and the pièce de résistance—a Hershey bar with almonds. I can still see down into that bag.

Other occasions brought almonds in every incarnation: chocolate-covered almonds from the famed Bissinger's chocolate shop; croissants with almond filling; marzipan fruits from the Swiss bakery; Giuliana's mother's almond crostata; Marcona almonds at my parents' cocktail time. There were sugar-covered almonds in soft pastel colors at Easter, and silvery ones at Christmas. Santa left unshelled almonds in the toe of my Christmas stocking; as I opened them with the mouth of our German nutcracker, I had no idea they had once been covered with a furry green hull. And I remember my mother teaching me how to brown slivered almonds in butter, watching them closely, so they didn't burn.

Many years after all those first tastes of almonds, I visited an almond orchard for the first time—a truly glorious experience. The ribbon-like rows wrapped the hills in every direction for miles. Once my love affair with almonds began, it could not help but spill over into so many other interests. Take bees, for example. Almond trees are completely dependent on bees for pollination. No bees, no almonds. Fortunately, bees travel well. They arrive in almond country by the truckful, during fertilization season—from Modesto to Sacramento in Northern California, and near Bakersfield in the southern part of the state. Some come north, traveling just half a day, but for others, it's a longer journey. Driving on an interstate highway between Texas and California in February, thinking about a hike down the Grand Canyon, one has no idea that the eighteen-wheelers in the next lane are transporting pollinators-for-hire, speeding through Nevada like fertility gods to the almond groves.

My friendship with almonds has led me to play in the kitchen, substituting almonds for pecans, cashews, and just about any other nut, using almond flour and almond milk in my baking instead of wheat flours or dairy milk, and enjoying almond butter as a replacement for peanut butter. Slivered or sliced, raw or roasted, ground or extracted, almonds have a rich range of textures, flavors, and uses: from amaretto and marzipan to amandine. Though they have been part of my daily snack routine for years (I've always kept a stash of almonds and dried apricots in my car or purse), I'm still discovering new ways to enjoy them. And I know I'm not alone in loving almonds. The world is catching on to not only how wonderful almonds taste, but also how good they are for you.

As I worked on this book over the last few years, the wonders of almonds unfolded all around me. When I travel, I keep my eye out for almonds. After a fifteen-year absence, I returned to Rome last fall with two of my children. The Coliseum now has educational displays in glass cases, one of which contains remnants of what was said to be a snack food sold at the equivalent of a concession stand: chicken bones (hot wings back then?) and almond shells! I pictured myself in a toga, munching on the same treat that I carried in my purse.

My daughter and I also spent time in France, exploring the mountainside villages that overlook the Mediterranean coast. Whenever I visit a city I make time to peruse the open-air markets, bringing home the local produce—in my camera. I loved discovering, as I traveled from village to village (Èze, Antibes, Saint-Paul-de-Vence, Beaulieu-sur-Mer), that every town market had freshly picked almonds, still in their green, fuzzy hulls. The markets are full of beautiful scenes and still lifes, some of which I share in this book. No wonder almonds are included in so many paintings of feasts; they've always been part of the European palate!

This project has been a labor of love for the creative team. We wanted to make a book that celebrates almonds and shares the beauty of their growing cycle, their rich cultural history and culinary traditions, and their presence in fine art, poetry, mythology, etymology, and even murder mysteries! These recipes from eighteen countries are a testament to the great variety of ways almonds can be enjoyed. We hope we have done justice to the noble, ancient almond. We trust that you will find much to savor here.

—Barbara Bryant

THE ESSENTIAL ALMOND

"My signor Ludovico and his court gobble up all the sculptures I give them," a pained teenaged Leonardo da Vinci protested in 1470, in his *Notes on Cuisine*. Employed by the court of Milan, the Renaissance genius was referring not to marble statuary but to sculptures he crafted from marzipan.

"Now I am determined," Leonardo continued, "to find other means that do not taste as good, so that my works may survive." While his *The Last Supper* and *Mona Lisa* have become icons in the history of art, Leonardo's former medium, a blend of sugar and almonds, has also survived as a favorite of bakers and dessert lovers for almost fifteen hundred years.

Heralded for its many attractive properties even thousands of years before Leonardo sculpted his perishable masterpieces, the almond is rich in nutrients, steeped in history, a favorite subject of poets and painters, and esteemed as a symbol of love and beauty. Its versatility in cooking, its "superfood" status, and its abundance are only some of the reasons to savor and appreciate the most celebrated of tree nuts. Indeed, cracking open the subject of almonds is an exciting voyage of discovery.

ANATOMY OF A NUT

We think of almonds as nuts, but scientists know them as the seeds of a tree in the rose family, the only edible part being the stone-like nut, covered by a pale, perforated shell. An almond yields willingly; its shell is easier to pry open than those of rock-hard walnuts and pecans or thumb-numbing pistachios.

While still attached to the tree, the almond is called a drupe, easily recognized by its fuzzy, gray-green hull. When the hull matures, it separates along a suture opening. Drupes are not unique to almonds. Coffee beans, olives, and all members of the genus *Prunus*—including apricots, cherries, and plums—produce these same fuzzy casings. Stone-fruit relatives also show their family resemblance to almonds by giving off a similar fragrance. Like cherry, peach, and apricot trees, almond trees array themselves in an extravaganza of pink and white blossoms in springtime, especially in places with mild winters and long, dry summers, such as California.

Unable to self-pollinate, almonds depend entirely on honeybees to carry pollen from male to female trees. Growers bring in hives every spring and rely on the bees' diligence: when conditions are right, a single colony can visit up to 500 million flowers.

ALMONDS AND BEES

It's no small feat to pollinate more than 800,000 acres of almonds. But that is what needs to happen every year to sustain 80 percent of the world's almond production in California. The vast number of almond orchards between Red Bluff and Bakersfield that need pollinating over a twenty-two-day period is too big of a job for local bees. The importation of more than half of all the honeybees in the United States is necessary to get the job done.

That's where the bee brokers come in. Each year beginning in mid-January, they start brokering bee rentals between almond growers and beekeepers for the February pollination season. Nearly 1.5 million beehives—or 40 billion bees, most of them driven cross-country on the backs of semi trucks—are required for the job. When brokers first started in 1973, hives were rented to almond growers at about $10 a hive. Today, prices are as high as $200 per colony.

Twenty thousand other species of bees pollinate plants, as do moths, wasps, butterflies, birds, and bats. But honeybees are one of the few pollinators that live socially, making them portable companions for humans.

The mechanics of pollination have remained the same throughout the years. Though almond growers use sophisticated agricultural technology, the harvest still relies on a simple visit from the bees. Ironically, the honey that the bees make from almond blossoms is amazingly bitter.

In recent years, colony collapse disorder has made the business of growing almonds even more precarious. It has destroyed colonies at a rate of about 30 percent a year, and before that losses were about 15 percent a year from pests and diseases. In recent years, the Almond Board of California has invested $1.4 million into bee health research and looked into alternatives to reduce the growers' reliance on the volatile honeybee population.

One of its alternatives is the so-called "self-compatible" almond tree, which is able to set nuts using pollen transferred among its own flowers and so requires fewer bees. Research teams are also looking into a solitary species of bees called blue orchard, which could supplement the honeybee workforce. The trade group is also recommending that growers plant forage that will help sustain the bees before and after pollination. Conservationists would like to see flowers planted in and around the almond groves, perhaps as hedgerows, to attract a bee population during other parts of the year. Increasing the diversity of crops would also enhance the bee population.

While the expansion of California nut acreage and production continues to set records, it looks like the honeybees have their work cut out for them for years to come.

—BLAKE HALLANAN, *journalist*

GREEN ALMONDS

"Do you have them yet?" That's the question almond growers and vendors at farmers markets hear every year in early spring. When you see chefs, food writers, and food-lovers congregating around a stall with boxes of what look like flattened, felt-covered olives, you know it's the season for green almonds—fuzzy green immature nuts with a gel-like interior.

From Bakersfield to Beirut, these embryonic almonds, available for only a few weeks from April to June, are considered a delicacy. With a distinct flavor that has been described as grassy, or fruity like guava, green almonds are less like a nut than a vegetable: crunchy, tangy, and something like a raw green bean. The entire fruit is edible, often dipped in salt and oil and eaten as a snack in Mediterranean and Middle Eastern countries.

As the fruit ripens and the exterior hardens, the young nuts can be pried out of their hulls like edamame or English peas in the pod. The soft kernels can be sautéed or added to a stew or used as a garnish. However green almonds are used, they are the culinary epitome of springtime. Look for them in farmers markets and shops that specialize in Middle Eastern foods.

Green almonds should be washed just before they are consumed or used in cooking. Keep the unwashed fruit in a bag in the refrigerator, and use it within a week. They may last even longer, but when you've waited all year, why wait to enjoy them?

CULTIVATION THROUGH THE AGES

Evidence abounds that almonds were part of ancient civilizations. The earliest-known almonds were found on the shore of the Sea of Galilee, thought to have been there more than nineteen thousand years ago. What are probably domesticated almonds—those bred for specific characteristics—have been found in Jordan and date to the Bronze Age (3300-1200 BCE). Although found along the Levant, or the eastern Mediterranean, the almond by origin is an Asiatic tree, whose first ancestors took root along the lower mountain slopes and in the deserts of central and southwestern Asia. Their sweet progeny flourished in regions known today as Turkmenistan, Uzbekistan, Tajikistan, Kyrgyzstan, Iran, Iraq, and Afghanistan. From here, almond cultivation spread around the Mediterranean; into present-day Turkey, Syria, and the Caucasus; and as far east as the Hindu Kush and Tian Shan, or the "Celestial Mountains," of China. The Silk Road, used by traders for two thousand years in their travels between Europe and Asia, passed through almond groves.

Throughout Mesopotamia, tree worship was common; Hebrew literature dating from 2000 BCE mentions the existence of almonds in Canaan. Both almond trees and their fruit appear in the Old Testament. In the book of Genesis, Jacob's hungry sons are sent to Egypt to procure grain from their brother Joseph. They offer him in trade "some of the choice fruits of the land ... a little balm and a little honey, gum, resin, pistachio nuts, and almonds." At the time, almond trees flourished in Israel, but not in Egypt, so the gift of the nut was highly regarded. In the book of Exodus, the story of Moses features almond branches as miraculous signs of priestly anointing, and an almond branch became the design model for the menorah: "Three cups, shaped like almond blossoms, were on one branch, with a knob and a flower ..."

Through the Israelites, almonds spread to Egypt. When King Tutankhamun was buried in a golden coffin in 322 BCE, his worshippers stuffed it with all kinds of treasures—splendid vases, jewelry, carved jackals, chariots, and the boy-king's mesmerizing gold and lapis mask. The 1922 discovery of the tomb revealed not only the exotic contents of the burial chamber, but also evidence of plant life: almonds, along with wheat, coriander, fenugreek, dates, and grapes, had been packed into baskets for the king in the afterlife.

And it looks like the king may have worn the by-products of almonds as well. Egyptians used almond oil to make perfumes and cosmetics. Kohl eyeliner, whose recipe included burned almonds, was believed to protect male and female wearers from evil spirits and improve failing eyesight.

Almonds secured a place in Greek and Roman culture and appear in the works of Homer and Virgil. *Apicius*, a collection of ancient Roman recipes and one of the world's oldest cookbooks, describes a sauce used on the Roman table: "Make a hot sauce for roast boar thus," it instructs, by crushing "pepper, cumin, celery seed, mint, thyme, satury [savory], saffron, toasted nuts, or toasted almonds, honey, broth, vinegar, and a little oil." Several centuries later, the Moors arrived in Toledo, Spain, and drove the Visigoths from the capital city, introducing sweets made with almonds. Toledo claims to be the home of marzipan, which eventually found its way into Leonardo da Vinci's studio.

On the European continent, almonds were most certainly part of the medieval diet. A fourteenth-century French recipe for blancmange mixed almond milk from ground blanched almonds with a broth made from capons. Another medieval manuscript instructed cooks to boil almond milk,

add a little vinegar, spread the mixture on a cloth with some sugar, and "when it is cold, gather it together, slice it, and serve it forth." Other recipes from a medieval cookbook feature almonds with pigeon, in a chicken and lemon dish, and as a key flavor in tarts and pastries. Ground almonds were used as a thickener for soups and stews. Almonds also appear in medieval medicines and cures.

At about this same time, the Cypriot King Peter II presented a syrup called *soumádha* as a gift to Poland's Casimir the Great. Soumádha is similar to orgeat—a mixture of almonds, sugar, and orange flower or rose water. (Orgeat is still served in Tunisia at wedding and engagement parties as a symbol of joy and purity because of its white color and fresh, flowery flavor.)

Continuing into the Renaissance and beyond, almonds became a common food in the cuisines, art, and customs of Europe and, through Franciscan friars, eventually found their way to the New World. In California, they found such a hospitable climate that now more than 80 percent of the world's supply is grown there. While no longer the stuff of afterlife fare, almonds continue to be celebrated in modern times. Amid the grasslands, California poppies, and purple clover of the Central Valley, the annual Capay Valley Almond Festival takes place in Yolo County, where booths offer almond baked goods and festival activities include an Almond Queen pageant and a baking contest. The blossoming almond trees of five Northern California towns are showcased during the festival along a twenty-one-mile "Blossom Trail." While it is dramatically shorter than the Silk Road, like it, the trail is a reminder of the almond tree's captivating beauty for those on the road.

Above: An ancient Roman feast depicted in *Les Saturnales,* Antoine-Francois Callet, c. 1800; antique wooden marzipan mold from Toledo, Spain, displaying Moorish architecture.

ALMONDS IN LEGEND, LANGUAGE, LITERATURE, AND ART

Few members of the plant kingdom surpass almonds for significance in legend and lore. The tree and its delicately fragrant blossoms and fruit have symbolized love, beauty, abundance, fertility, blessing, and authority.

Almonds were depicted in works of art as long ago as the reign of the Egyptian pharaohs, when an unknown artist painted the walls of a tomb to show a man holding the nut. Continuing in the Middle Ages, almonds and almond trees appeared in illuminated manuscripts in Europe and the Middle East. In medieval and Renaissance art, almonds became a symbol of the Virgin's purity; the *mandorla*—"almond" in Italian—refers to an oval or almond-shaped aureola that often surrounds both Mary and Jesus in Christian art.

Later, celebrated artists such as Giovanna Garzoni, Edouard Manet, Pierre Auguste Renoir, and Vincent van Gogh featured almonds and almond trees in paintings, and the almond drupe, seed, shell, and blossoms appear in botanical illustrations by Elizabeth Blackwell, A.W. Mumford, and others.

Poets and novelists also have extolled almonds and associated them with love, hope, and happiness. Virgil regarded a profusely blooming almond tree as a predictor of a good year: "Mark, too, when in the woods the almond clothes herself richly in blossom and bends her fragrant boughs; if the fruit prevails, the corn crops will keep pace with it, and a great threshing come with a great heat." Sir Edwin Arnold, the nineteenth-century English poet, is inspired by spring's early flowering trees in "Almond Blossom":

> *Blossom of the almond trees,*
> *April's gift to April's bees,*
> *Birthday ornament of Spring,*
> *Flora's fairest daughterling . . .*

Above: Detail from wall painting in ancient Egyptian tomb; almond-shaped mandorla surrounding the Virgin Mary in *Virgin in Glory*, Pinturicchio, c. 1500.

Twentieth-century Greek writer Nikos Kazantzakis conjures up the fantastic in his almond references: "I said to the almond tree, 'Sister, speak to me of God.' And the almond tree blossomed." More recently, the American poet Louise Glück, in her collection *The Seven Ages*, found "Desire, loneliness, wind in the flowering almond."

SWEET, BITTER, AND SYNTHETIC

This enduring symbol of love and beauty also has a dark side: the bitter almond has been known for two thousand years to be poisonous. The bitter almond, like the kernel of a peach, cherry, or apricot, when crushed or chewed releases water-soluble hydrocyanic acid, or HCN, the lethal ingredient in cyanide, and benzaldehyde, which carries the heavenly fragrance of almonds and is toxic only in large amounts. As few as ten bitter almonds can make someone sick, yet they are still sought after as an ingredient in certain traditional recipes, such as Italian amaretti cookies.

The good news is that since bitter almonds are not grown commercially in the United States and their marketing is strictly limited, we are unlikely to ever come across them here, except in murder mysteries, where their by-product, cyanide, makes regular appearances. Mystery fans know that if the corpse smells of almonds, the scent is a telltale marker for cyanide poisoning. The toxin was Agatha Christie's most frequent poison-of-choice and appeared in four novels, including the aptly titled *Sparkling Cyanide*.

For most flavoring extracts, cooks prize purity and extraction directly from the original plant. Almonds are the exception. An authentic-smelling synthetic extract made from benzaldehyde can be made in a lab, resulting in an almond extract that is inexpensive and tastes as good as the "pure" form.

WORLD ALMOND PRODUCTION: CALIFORNIA LEADS THE WAY

The state of California produces most of the world's almond crop. Australia and the European Union countries are a distant second and third, followed by Turkey, Iran, and Tunisia leading the remaining producers. The U.S. exports about 70 percent of its almond crop, primarily to India and China.

California	80%
Australia	6%
EU-27	6%
Turkey	1%
Tunisia	1%
Iran	1%
Chile	1%
Morocco	1%
China	<1%
Syria	<1%
Others	2%

Almond farming and production in early twentieth-century California

The Cultivated Almond

To Almonds, California Is Paradise

California's Central Valley was made for almond orchards: long summers, mild winters, moderate rain, abundant sunshine, and deep, loamy soils are ideal growing conditions. The long valley, which forms a cradle between the Sierra Nevada mountain range to the east and the Pacific Coast ranges to the west, was once an enormous lake. Today, rivers flow from the Sierra to the valley floor. Day-to-night temperature swings average 25 degrees, and the sun shines three hundred days a year.

We have Franciscan friars to thank for introducing the almond tree to California from Spain in the mid-1700s, as they traveled the state establishing missions in coastal areas from San Diego to Sonoma. By the 1800s, intrepid farmers realized almond trees would do better in a Mediterranean climate and planted them inland. The first recognized almond orchard in the state, along the Bear River in the Sacramento Valley, was planted in 1843.

In the next decade, nurseries in California were selling almond trees, many of them supplied by Felix Gillet, a French nurseryman in Nevada City. The commercial industry really took off once farmers tinkered with details. In Suisun, southwest of Sacramento, A.T. Hatch planted two thousand seedlings in 1879, to limited success. He subsequently took four of the heartiest rootstocks and planted them close together to aid in the pollination process. He named them Nonpareil, IXL, Ne Plus Ultra, and La Prima. Planted together, the trees grew well, and Hatch's success was repeated by others in the Sacramento Valley. His selection of varieties is considered the beginning of the California almond industry. Today, almonds are the golden state's biggest commercial crop and its top agricultural export, with 810,000 acres under production.

Of the hundreds of almond cultivars developed since Gillet's successes in perennial agriculture, twenty-five major varieties are grown today in

California, most of them in the Central Valley. The state produces virtually all of the domestic supply of almonds.

The major almond varieties grown today fall into three broad groups: Nonpareil, California, and Mission. Nonpareil (non-par-EL, from French "without equal") almonds, the most popular, are harvested early. They are easily blanched and cut, and are thought of as the "king" of snacking almonds. They also make up the largest percentage of California's almond production.

Several varieties make up the California group, including Monterey, Fritz, Sonora, Peerless, and Price almonds. They are harvested after Nonpareils. The Mission group includes Butte, Padre, and Mission varieties, among others. Smaller than other almonds, with full-bodied flavor and dark, wrinkled skins that flavorings adhere well to, they make good additions to recipes.

Almonds are significant to California's annual economy: some 70 percent of the state's total crop—the top U.S. specialty crop export, worth $2.8 billion— is exported to ninety countries. India and China are the biggest customers.

Through the Year with Almonds

A year in the life of an almond begins after the spring bloom. If spring rains and wind are moderate and blossoms are undisturbed, young almonds form on the branches by early summer. Shells develop, encased in fuzzy hulls, which dry out in the summer sun around July and split along one side to reveal the shells. Inside, the nuts begin to dry before ripening and falling to the ground.

Harvest ranges from early August to November. The traditional method, still practiced on small farms, is to lay tarpaulins beneath the trees and knock the almonds off with sticks and rubber mallets. Workers then drag tarps brimming with almonds into clearings, rake them each day so that they dry, and shovel them into bags before taking them to a processing facility.

On many large farms, mechanized "shakers" grip a tree and shake its trunk. After the nuts dry, a sweeper moves them into rows, and a harvester collects them, removing leaves and dirt. The crop is taken to an elevator, weighed, and sent to a facility where the almonds are cleaned and hulled.

After being fumigated for insects and fed through a machine to remove foreign material, the almonds are trucked to a processing plant where the

nuts are sized and graded, offered to buyers from all over the world, and finally prepared for shipping.

By November, a drive along Interstate 5 in the Central Valley reveals heaps of dry almond hulls resembling mountain peaks, their tawny color capable of camouflaging a pride of lions. In another month, the mountains will be moved—put out to bid and sold to livestock-feed manufacturers. No part of the almond goes to waste.

After harvest, the trees settle in for a well-deserved rest. Their branches are mostly bare except for early-appearing buds, whose growth the lower temperatures will slow. For three to four months the trees are dormant, and orchard activity focuses on pruning, mulching, and replanting. By the end of the year, the trees have dropped their leaves.

Early in January or February, the trees begin to bud again, sending out tender green leaves as the days grow longer. As spring approaches, buds change into pink and white flowers, and their spreading, open canopies fill the air with a woody, nutty fragrance. By mid-February, the vital honeybees have arrived, flown or driven in for pollination duty. For every acre of almonds, two hives are needed. By mid-March the bloom is over, the petals have fallen, and the beehives are gone. And the young almonds begin to form again.

Many of us consider nuts a forbidden food due to their high fat content. However, almonds also have a high protein content, along with other beneficial components such as healthy, cholesterol-lowering monounsaturated fats, making them especially nutritious. Almonds are a highly satiating food, partly because they're crunchy and scrumptious, but also because they're calorie dense. A snack of dry-roasted almonds can lead to the consumption of fewer calories at your next meal.

Almonds are a great source of:

• *Protein*: A quarter-cup (30 g) of almonds contains 7.62 grams—more protein than a large egg, which contains 6 grams.

• *Vitamin E (in alpha-tocopherol form)*: Research has found that when vitamin E is low, inflammation tends to be higher, and the body's immune response to threats is diminished. Getting more of this nutrient lowers inflammation and increases immune health, and may help reduce the risk of chronic disease.

• *Magnesium*: A single-ounce (30-g) snack of almonds provides about 25 percent of our daily need of magnesium, which may help protect against diabetes.

—Cheryl Forberg, R.D., chef, nutritionist for NBC's *The Biggest Loser*, and author of five *Biggest Loser* cookbooks

Nutrition and Versatility in a Nutshell

The Nutritional Value of Almonds

Hippocrates taught his students that food was medicine, and medicine, food: "A wise man should consider that health is the greatest of human blessings." A balanced diet that includes nuts—among other plant-based foods such as fruits, vegetables, seeds, and grains—protects against disease. Nuts are an excellent source of monounsaturated fats, which help regulate cholesterol levels and prevent cholesterol absorption. They serve us well as a source of antioxidants, which retard the aging process and protect against many diseases.

Almonds have gained their "superfood" status rightfully: compared to other tree nuts, they rank first in protein, fiber, calcium, vitamin E, riboflavin, and niacin. Plus, they deliver another startling property: even though a 1-ounce (30 g) serving has 160 calories, the body absorbs only 129 of those calories.

An ounce of almonds—or a handful of about two dozen nuts—contains 35 percent of the daily vitamin E requirement. Low levels of vitamin E are associated with age-related cognitive decline and poor memory performance—another reason to remember to eat an ounce of almonds a day. A study published in the *Journal of the American Medical Association* determined that participants in the group consuming the most vitamin E from food sources, instead of supplements, had a 67 percent lower risk of Alzheimer's disease than those whose intake was lowest. Besides being good for your brain, almonds are good for your bones. They have more bone-strengthening calcium—75 milligrams per ounce (30 g)—than all other nuts.

ALMONDS IN THE KITCHEN

Uniquely versatile, almonds are available in more forms than any other nut. They do not discolor, and they add texture, crunch, and a distinctive flavor to any dish you make. But how to keep them at their best? Squirrels know by instinct what we humans had to learn: nuts stored in their shells and kept cool will stay fresh longer. The more unsaturated fat a nut contains, the quicker air and moisture can turn it rancid.

Look for nuts with intact, closed shells. Almonds are at their delicious best when just harvested, so buy the freshest available. Almonds that have been chopped, blanched, or roasted, or those to which moisture has been added, have a shorter shelf life than almonds stored whole. And dry-roasted almonds last longer than those preserved in oil, such as chocolate-coated ones.

Store almonds in a tightly sealed jar and keep in a cool, dry spot out of the sun. Unshelled almonds will keep in the refrigerator for a year, or in the freezer for up to two years. With shells removed, almonds will last for four to five months in the refrigerator or for up to a year in the freezer.

Almond Products for the Pantry

• Shelled Whole Almonds can be used for just about anything. Buy whole almonds raw, skin intact, so you can blanch, roast, sliver, dice, chop, or grind them. Most raw almonds (with skins) are heat-treated (pasteurized).

• Blanched Almonds have been skinned. To blanch, immerse whole raw almonds in boiling water for 30 seconds, remove one, and test to see if the skin can be easily pinched off. If not, continue blanching for another 30 seconds or more, repeating the test. Drain and dry the nuts before using.

• Slivered Almonds are slender pieces of blanched almonds. In a stir-fry or grain dish, slivered almonds contribute crunch and flavor.

• Sliced or Flaked Almonds, with or without their mildly tannic skins, add eye appeal and a contrasting crunchiness to classic dishes such as green beans amandine or trout amandine. Use them in salads and as a topping for pastries and quick breads, such as muffins.

• Diced or Chopped Almonds are sold with or without skins and are used as a topping or an ingredient in baked goods, stuffings, and coatings for fish, chicken, or veal.

• Almond Flour is gluten-free and has more protein than wheat flour. Its texture is smooth and its flavor slightly sweet and buttery. It contains protein and fiber, plus antioxidants and calcium, and can be made at home by grinding *frozen* or *cold* blanched almonds in a food processor (nuts at room temperature will turn into almond butter when ground). Store in a sealed container in the refrigerator or freezer for up to several months.

*Descriptions of some almond products were provided in part by the Almond Board of California.

• ALMOND MEAL is coarser than almond flour and may contain the skins, so before substituting almond meal for almond flour, consider their differences. Almond meal can be used in a wide array of baked goods. It can replace up to one-half the volume of flour called for in a baking recipe, and can be used for breading meat, seafood, and vegetables.

• ALMOND PASTE AND MARZIPAN, both made from ground almonds and sugar, can be bought in cans or rolls to use in baked goods. Almond paste contains almonds, sugar, and a liquid. Marzipan is made by adding sugar and sometimes egg whites to almond paste, and is more pliable than paste. It is often tinted with colors and molded into whimsical shapes.

• ALMOND OIL is a light cooking oil with a high smoke point. A great alternative to butter, it is cholesterol-free and carries the flavor of the nut. Refined almond oil is mild tasting and suitable for frying, while cold-pressed almond oil adds a pleasantly strong flavor to a vinaigrette.

• ALMOND BUTTER is widely available and sold salted or unsalted, raw or roasted. Almond butter can also be prepared at home (see recipe, page 54).

• ALMOND MILK is made from ground almonds and water and is one of the most nutritious alternatives to cow's milk. Some of the brands available commercially contain vanilla or chocolate. Almond milk can also be prepared at home and has a light, subtle almond flavor (see recipe, page 56).

• ALMOND EXTRACTS are labeled "pure," "natural," or "imitation": all rely on some form of benzaldehyde for their flavor. Pure extract has benzaldehyde derived from bitter almonds; natural extract uses benzaldehyde derived from cassia bark, and imitation flavoring contains synthetic benzaldehyde.

The Global Almond

As a young country, the United States cannot claim almonds as part of its epic history as can many cultures explored in these pages—the stuff of ancient poets, kings, and Renaissance giants—but we *can* claim to joyfully delight in the glories and traditions of these long-standing cultures and, around the table at least, attempt to make them part of our own.

Many immigrants who come to America often carry nothing but memories of their native homes that are deeply rooted in their food, agricultural customs, and celebrations. This book is filled with recipes from around the world carried here from far lands. At the heart of the almond's history are cooks like you, serving their families and friends time-honored recipes with extra doses of taste, fun, and healthfulness. From the heights of chefs at royal courts to humbler hosts and guests sitting cross-legged on the floor, in every land where almonds grow or have carved out their place in culture the almond is an enduring and endearing part of world history. ℰ

Right (clockwise from top left): Women sorting harvested almonds in India; an almond mole vendor outside Mexico City; multicolored sugared almonds, Verdun, France; bins of almonds and dried fruit at a market in Marrakech; green almonds for sale at an outdoor market in southern France; colorful fruit-shaped marzipan confections in Paris.

STARTERS & SNACKS

ALMONDS AND CHEESE

Nuts in general, and almonds in particular, are one of my favorite companions for cheese. I don't have much of a sweet tooth, so I prefer a savory accompaniment to a sweet one. In the fall, I'll serve almonds in the shell, with a nutcracker, to accompany the cheese course, sometimes warming them in the oven first. And I always have a jar of toasted almonds in my pantry. I buy them with the skin on and toast them slowly for a long time—30 to 40 minutes at 325°F (160°C)—until they're caramel-colored inside and brittle. Some people may think they're overdone, but I like them dark and crunchy. Sometimes, if I'm serving blue cheese and sweet wine, I'll stir the toasted almonds into warm honey and spoon that alongside.

—Janet Fletcher, cooking instructor and author of *The Cheese Course*, *Cheese & Wine*, and *Cheese & Beer*

Spiced Roasted Almonds with Rosemary and Lemon

Spiced almonds roasted in the oven are a perfect hors d'oeuvre or snack. A fragrant blend of rosemary, lemon, and the kick of cayenne pepper gives these nuts their Mediterranean flavor. Serve the almonds warm; their flavor will diminish as they cool.

2 cups (8 oz/225 g) raw almonds

2 tablespoons extra virgin olive oil

1 tablespoon minced fresh rosemary

2 teaspoons salt, plus extra for sprinkling

2 teaspoons sweet Hungarian paprika

1 teaspoon finely grated lemon zest

½ teaspoon cayenne pepper

½ teaspoon freshly ground black pepper

½ teaspoon sugar

Preheat the oven to 350°F (180°C).

Place the almonds in a large bowl. Add all the remaining ingredients except the salt for sprinkling. Toss to coat. Spread in one layer on a rimmed baking sheet. Roast, shaking the pan once or twice, until golden brown and fragrant, about 15 minutes. Transfer to parchment paper to cool slightly.

Lightly sprinkle with salt. Serve warm.

MAKES 2 CUPS (225 g)

TOASTING WHOLE, CHOPPED, SLIVERED, OR SLICED ALMONDS

Place the almonds in a single layer on a roasting pan. Toast in a preheated 350°F (180°C) oven, turning them several times with a spatula, until golden brown, 10 to 15 minutes.

Salted and Spiced Green Almonds

Green almonds are the developing nuts on the almond tree. Their season is fleeting, a mere eight weeks between April and June, before the inner shell hardens. During this time, the entire nut is edible, from the fuzzy pod to the jelly-like interior, which hardens throughout the season. Green almonds are a favorite snack in the Middle East, served simply with salt to balance the young nuts' natural sourness. This recipe adds a little sugar and spice to the mix to ensure you'll come back for more.

Loquats, Almonds and a Rose, Giovanna Garzoni, c.1622

¼ cup (60 ml) extra virgin olive oil

¼ teaspoon sugar

Pinch of cayenne pepper

1 tablespoon sea salt

8 ounces (225 g) green almonds
(about 24), rinsed and dried

Whisk the oil, sugar, and cayenne together in a small serving bowl. Place the salt in another small serving bowl.

Using your fingers, dip an almond in the oil and then the salt. Eat the entire nut, including the pod.

SERVES 6 TO 8

Smoked Trout Mousse with Almonds

Smoked fish is a staple throughout Scandinavia, where smoking was originally used as a method of preserving fish and meat. Today, it is enjoyed as a flavorful delicacy, served on open-faced sandwiches, in fish patties, or simply straight from the harbor smokehouse with a squeeze of lemon. This fluffy mousse is simple to prepare yet elegant to serve. A garnish of almonds adds texture and toasted flavor to the smoky fish.

MOUSSE

8 ounces (225 g) smoked trout, skin and any bones removed

4 ounces (115 g) cream cheese, at room temperature

¼ cup (60 g) sour cream

¼ cup (60 g) grated onion

3 tablespoons fresh lemon juice

1 teaspoon Worcestershire sauce

1 teaspoon freshly ground black pepper

½ teaspoon Tabasco sauce

Thinly sliced European-style pumpernickel squares, baguette slices, or crudités for serving

½ cup (2 oz/60 g) slivered almonds, toasted (see page 41)

Minced fresh dill for garnish

To make the mousse, combine all of the ingredients in a food processor. Process until the consistency is light and smooth. If too thick, add additional sour cream. Transfer to a serving bowl. Serve immediately or cover and refrigerate for up to 2 days.

To serve as canapés, spoon a dollop of mousse on pumpernickel squares or smear on baguette slices. Sprinkle with slivered almonds and garnish with dill. To serve family style, scatter the almonds and dill over the mousse and serve with baguette slices or crudités on the side for dipping.

MAKES ABOUT 1½ CUPS (460 g)

Burnt Sugar Almonds

Open-air Christmas markets are held throughout Germany in December during Advent. Stalls line the streets selling handmade gifts, decorations and holiday treats, including gebrannte mandeln, *burnt sugar almonds. The nuts are cooked fresh in copper kettles, and the aromas of cinnamon, sugar, and almonds waft through the air, proving impossible to resist. Burnt sugar almonds may also be prepared at home, and they make lovely holiday gifts. A sprinkle of sea salt will coax further nibbling— not that you need an excuse.*

1 cup (225 g) plus ⅓ cup (75 g) sugar, divided

⅓ cup (75 ml) water

1 teaspoon ground cinnamon

2 cups (8 oz/225 g) raw almonds

1 teaspoon pure vanilla extract

Sea salt, for sprinkling (optional)

Line a rimmed baking sheet with parchment paper.

Add the 1 cup (225 g) sugar, the water, and cinnamon to a large, heavy saucepan (not nonstick) and stir to combine. Bring to a boil over medium-high heat. Add the almonds and stir constantly until the water evaporates and the sugar begins to dry out.

Reduce the heat to medium and keep stirring until the sugar begins to melt and the almonds begin to brown and have a shiny coat. Add the ⅓ cup (75 g) sugar and the vanilla and keep stirring. The almonds will begin to snap, crackle, and pop. (This is normal; the almonds are releasing their water.)

Continue stirring until the sugar is half melted and the almonds are shiny and lumpy. Pour the almonds onto the prepared baking sheet. Do not touch them; they will be very hot. Sprinkle with sea salt, if using. Separate the almonds with a wooden spoon as they cool. Let cool completely. Store in an airtight container at room temperature for up to 3 weeks.

MAKES ABOUT 2 CUPS (225 g)

Almond-Stuffed Dates with Bacon

Bowls of dried fruit and nuts welcome visitors to homes throughout North Africa and the Middle East. These plump stuffed dates with a decidedly American twist take inspiration from that gracious custom. The dates are filled with crunchy toasted almonds nestled in creamy spiced goat cheese, then wrapped in bacon and crisped in the oven. Since the Medjool variety is extremely sweet, choose the smallest in size so that their sweetness and texture will not overpower the other ingredients.

24 small Medjool dates

1 cup (8 oz/225 g) fresh white goat cheese at room temperature

½ teaspoon finely grated orange zest

¼ teaspoon cayenne pepper

Pinch of salt

24 raw almonds (1 oz/30 g), toasted (see page 41)

12 slices bacon, halved crosswise, about 1 pound (450 g)

Preheat the oven to 475°F (245°C).

Cut a small slit down the center of each date and carefully remove the pit while keeping the date intact as much as possible.

Whisk the goat cheese, zest, cayenne, and salt together in a small bowl until smooth. Using a teaspoon, stuff each date with the cheese mixture until the cavity is nearly full. Insert an almond in the center of the cheese.

Wrap a bacon slice around the middle of each date and arrange them on a broiler pan, seam side down, without overcrowding. Bake until the bacon is crisp, about 15 minutes. Let cool slightly before serving (the cheese will be very hot). Insert a toothpick into each date and serve warm.

MAKES 24 PIECES

Green Olive and Almond Tapenade

The word tapenade *comes from the Provençal word for capers, and as its name suggests, tapenade often includes capers, as well as olives, anchovies, and oil in a pungent, briny paste redolent of the south of France. What sets this recipe apart is the almonds, which balance the feistiness of the anchovies and olives, smoothing the flavor. Use as a condiment to spread on bread, sprinkle over pizza and pasta, or garnish grilled fish and chicken.*

2 cups (225 g) pitted green olives

½ cup (2 oz/60 g) raw almonds, toasted (see page 41)

3 anchovies in oil, drained

1 large clove garlic

1 tablespoon extra virgin olive oil

2 teaspoons capers, drained and rinsed

1 teaspoon freshly ground black pepper

Place all of the ingredients in a food processor. Process to a coarse paste. Serve at room temperature or cover and refrigerate for up to 2 days.

MAKES ABOUT 2½ CUPS (285 g)

Still Life and Blossoming Almond Trees, Diego Rivera, 1931

ALMONDS IN PROVENCE

Almonds have long been cultivated in Provence and figure large in the pastry and sauces of the region as well as in holiday traditions. *Casse-dents,* literally "teeth-breakers," hard biscuits similar to biscotti, are still made from scratch in traditional homes in Provence, even though the biscuits are available at nearly any village *pâtisserie.* Tasting more of nuts than sugar, *casse-dents* are served for dipping into sweet wine as an aperitif. A combination of bitter and sweet almonds flavors the *crème pâtisserie* that fills sweet pastries. Ground almonds are used to thicken sauces and tapenades, while toasted slivered almonds are sprinkled over the classic dish *truite aux amandes.*

Almonds are also an essential ingredient in the traditional thirteen desserts served on Christmas Eve in Provence. They are one of the *quatre mendiants,* or four beggars (walnuts or hazelnuts, raisins, dried figs, and almonds, which represent the four mendicant monastic orders: Dominicans, Augustinians, Franciscans, and Carmelites) and are served mixed together on a plate or scattered on the table. *Nougat aux noix,* made with almonds and honey, is another essential component of the meal. Although the acreage of the nut in Provence is declining, the traditional uses of almonds remain embedded in the culture of the region.

—GEORGEANNE BRENNAN, author of
The Food and Flavors of Haute Provence
and *Savoring France*

White Gazpacho with Green Grapes and Almonds

White gazpacho is a classic dish from Spain dating back to the Moorish occupation of Andalusia in medieval times. This cool and creamy version includes toasted almonds, green grapes, thick yogurt, olive oil, and garlic. It's a light and refreshing soup, perfect for a summer day. If you can find new green almonds at your market between April and June, they may be used as a garnish. The consistency of the soup will be thin, so serve it in shallow bowls to showcase the grape and almond garnish.

Fruits on a Table, Edouard Manet, 1864

1 English cucumber, peeled and coarsely chopped

1 cup (180 g) seedless green grapes, plus 8 for garnish

2 cloves garlic

1 cup (225 g) Greek-style whole-milk yogurt

¼ cup (60 ml) fresh lemon juice

1 teaspoon salt

1 teaspoon red wine vinegar

¼ teaspoon Tabasco sauce

¼ cup (1 oz/30 g) raw almonds, toasted (see page 41) and chopped

Extra virgin olive oil, for drizzling

Puree the cucumber in a blender or food processor. Push through a fine-mesh sieve into a bowl. Puree the 1 cup (180 g) grapes and the garlic in the blender or food processor. Push through a fine-mesh sieve into the bowl with the cucumber.

Whisk the yogurt, lemon juice, salt, vinegar, and Tabasco into the soup. Taste and adjust the seasoning. Cover and refrigerate for at least 2 hours or overnight before serving.

To serve, slice the 8 grapes in half crosswise and scatter over the soup. Sprinkle with almonds and drizzle with a little olive oil. Serve immediately.

MAKES ABOUT 2¹/₂ CUPS (625 ml) SOUP; SERVES 2 TO 3

Almond Butter Granola Bars

Homemade granola bars are a healthy snack and remarkably easy to prepare. You can pick and choose favorite ingredients while omitting excess sugars, fat, additives, and allergens such as peanuts. These bars are packed with almonds and studded with raisins and dried cranberries, adding protein and natural sweetness. Apricots or dates can be substituted for the raisins and dried cranberries.

1¾ cups (145 g) old-fashioned oats

¾ cup (3 oz/90 g) sliced almonds

½ cup (60 g) unsweetened
   grated coconut

¼ cup (20 g) raw wheat germ

⅓ cup (75 ml) brown rice syrup

2 tablespoons honey

⅓ cup (90 g) unsalted almond butter
   (see page 54)

2 tablespoons grapeseed oil

1 teaspoon vanilla extract

1 teaspoon ground cinnamon

½ teaspoon salt

1 cup (180 g) raisins

½ cup (60 g) dried cranberries

Preheat the oven to 350°F (180°C). Oil a 9 by 12-inch (23 by 30-cm) baking pan. Line with parchment paper and oil the parchment.

Toss the oats, almonds, coconut, and wheat germ in a bowl. Pour onto a rimmed baking sheet and spread evenly. Bake until fragrant and lightly toasted, 8 to 10 minutes. Remove from the oven and transfer to a bowl. Reduce the oven temperature to 300°F (150°C).

Gently heat the syrup and honey in a small saucepan over medium-low heat until runny. Remove from the heat and whisk in the almond butter, oil, vanilla, cinnamon, and salt. Pour over the oats, mixing to thoroughly combine. Stir in the dried fruit. Pour into the prepared pan, spreading evenly.

Bake until golden brown, 30 to 35 minutes. Remove and let cool completely in the pan until firm, at least 2 hours. Cut into squares or rectangles. Store in an airtight container for up to 1 week.

MAKES ABOUT 24 BARS

ALMONDS IN THE RESTAURANT PANTRY

Almonds are indispensable to the pantries at both of my restaurants, Picholine and Artisanal Bistro. At Picholine we roast Marcona almonds with olive oil and spices, and serve them with warm olives as an appetizer. It's always nice to have a nut on the cheese board—with almonds I serve fresh goat and unaged sheep cheeses. And when in season, I love to serve green almonds in the husk.

In general, I like to serve almonds plain, because I don't want to interfere with flavor profiles. I use them in tandem with classical culinary traditions—so if I'm making a Moroccan dish, or a Catalan-influenced one with a romesco-style sauce, I'll reach for almonds for authenticity. I love using nut purees as a binding agent, so not only will I mix almonds with anchovies for an antipasto, I'll also use almond flour to thicken my sauces. As for our dessert offerings, almonds are the star ingredient in financiers, macaroons, tarts and cakes.

—TERRANCE BRENNAN, chef, Picholine and Artisanal Bistro, New York City, and author of *Artisanal Cooking: A Chef Shares His Passion for Handcrafting Great Meals at Home*

ALMOND BUTTER

3 cups (12 oz/350 g) raw whole almonds
Pinch of sea salt (optional)

Preheat the oven to 350°F (180°C). Spread the almonds on a rimmed baking sheet. Roast, shaking the pan once or twice, until fragrant, 12 to 14 minutes. Remove and let cool for 2 minutes.

Transfer the almonds to a food processor. Add salt, if using. Process until the almonds begin to stick together, about 8 minutes, scraping the sides down every few minutes. Continue to process until a grainy butter forms, about 2 more minutes. Adjust the amount of salt to taste. For a creamy butter, process an additional 4 to 5 minutes. Transfer to an airtight container and store in the refrigerator for up to 3 months.

MAKES ABOUT 1¹/₂ CUPS (340 g)

Almond and Raisin Granola

Homemade granola is a cinch to make, and a wonderful way to use up odds and ends in your pantry. It's also a perfect solution to dietary restrictions, including gluten intolerance or peanut allergies. Tinker with it to your taste by substituting favorite grains and seeds, dried fruits, and nuts. This granola mix is brimming with almonds, which add a protein boost and an assertive crunch. Wait until the end to add the raisins, as they may burn while baking.

2 cups (180 g) old-fashioned oats

1 cup (4 oz/115 g) raw almonds, coarsely chopped

¼ cup (30 g) unsweetened grated coconut

¼ cup (20 g) raw wheat germ

1 teaspoon ground cinnamon

½ teaspoon salt

¼ cup (60 ml) grapeseed oil

2 tablespoons honey

2 tablespoons maple syrup

2 tablespoons brown sugar

½ teaspoon vanilla extract

½ cup (90 g) raisins

Preheat the oven to 300°F (150°C). Line a rimmed baking sheet with parchment paper.

Toss the oats, almonds, coconut, wheat germ, cinnamon, and salt in a large bowl.

Whisk the oil, honey, maple syrup, brown sugar, and vanilla in a small saucepan over medium-low heat until the sugar dissolves. Pour over the oats and toss to thoroughly coat.

Spread the granola on the prepared baking sheet. Bake, jiggling the pan once or twice, until the granola is toasted golden brown, about 30 minutes. Remove and let cool.

Break up any large clumps in the granola. Mix in the raisins. Store in an airtight container for up to 1 week.

MAKES ABOUT 4 CUPS (350 g)

Banana-Almond Smoothie

This dairy-free smoothie makes a terrific breakfast drink or snack. The trick to this treat is to use frozen bananas. They make a rich and creamy purée while eliminating the need for ice cubes, which waters down the flavor. Freezing bananas is a great way to store them before they become too ripe. Peel the bananas and store in a freezer bag for up to 3 months.

1 large frozen banana, cut into chunks

1 cup (250 ml) unsweetened almond milk (recipe follows)

1 tablespoon unsalted creamy almond butter (see page 54)

1 teaspoon honey or light brown sugar

¼ teaspoon vanilla extract

Pinch of ground cinnamon

Combine all of the ingredients and purée in a blender until smooth. Add additional honey or sugar, if desired. Serve immediately.

SERVES 1

UNSWEETENED ALMOND MILK

1 cup (4 oz/115 g) raw almonds

3 cups (750 ml) water

Soak the almonds in water to cover overnight. Drain. Purée the almonds and the water in a blender or food processor for 1 minute. Strain through a sieve lined with cheesecloth. Discard the solids. Transfer to an airtight container and refrigerate for up to 3 days.

SWEETENED ALMOND MILK

To sweeten the almond milk, add 2 pitted Medjool dates or 2 tablespoons honey and ½ teaspoon vanilla extract to the drained nuts and water before puréeing.

MAKES ABOUT 3 CUPS (750 ml)

Almond Chai with Dates and Honey

Chai *literally means "tea," but it's often used to refer to flavorful Masala chai, an Indian and South Asian tea preparation with spices and milk. In this recipe, almond milk and dates impart aroma and natural sweetness while the tea steeps. If desired, honey may be added for additional sweetness.*

1½ cups (375 ml) water

4 cloves

3 cardamom pods, crushed

2 Medjool dates

1 cinnamon stick

1-inch (2.5-cm) piece fresh ginger, thinly sliced

½ teaspoon black peppercorns

1½ cups (375 ml) unsweetened almond milk (see page 56)

1 tablespoon black tea (such as Darjeeling, Assam, or English Breakfast)

Honey (optional)

Combine the water, cloves, cardamom, dates, cinnamon, ginger, and peppercorns in a medium saucepan. Bring to a boil, then reduce the heat to a simmer. Partially cover and cook for 10 minutes. Add the almond milk and tea. Simmer, partially covered, for 5 minutes. Add honey to taste, if desired. Strain into warm mugs. Serve immediately.

SERVES 2 TO 3

Almond Branches in Bloom, Vincent van Gogh, 1890

SALADS & VEGETABLES

Asian Citrus and Almond Slaw

Sliced almonds are perfectly at home in crispy coleslaws. They add a delicate nutty note to the tangle of cabbage, peppers, and carrots. In this light Asian coleslaw, citrus juice and sesame oil replace mayonnaise, while ginger and chile add heat and bite.

DRESSING

1 clove garlic, minced

2 tablespoons rice wine vinegar

2 tablespoons fresh lime juice

2 tablespoons fresh orange juice

2 tablespoons Asian sesame oil

2 teaspoons finely grated fresh ginger with juice

1 teaspoon sugar

1 teaspoon salt, or to taste

½ teaspoon freshly ground black pepper

Dash of hot sauce (optional)

SLAW

4 green onions, white and green parts, thinly sliced on the diagonal

1 small head Savoy or green cabbage, cored and shredded

1 large carrot, peeled and julienned

1 red jalapeño or Fresno chile, minced

4 ounces (115 g) sugar snap peas, trimmed and thinly sliced on the diagonal

½ cup (20 g) chopped fresh cilantro

¼ cup (1 oz/30 g) sliced almonds

To make the dressing, whisk all the ingredients together in a small bowl.

Combine the green onions, cabbage, carrot, chile, and snap peas in a large bowl. Add the dressing. Toss to thoroughly coat. Let stand for 30 minutes, or cover and refrigerate for up to 2 hours. Before serving, stir in the cilantro and almonds.

SERVES 6 AS A SIDE DISH

White Peach and Prosciutto Salad with Green Almonds

Fragrant white peaches start coming into season in May, the same time that green almonds are available at farmers' markets and Mediterranean grocery stores. Mild and slightly tart, green almonds are the crowning touch on a sublime salad of sweet white peaches, salty prosciutto, and peppery arugula. If green almonds are not available, substitute toasted sliced almonds.

2 tablespoons fresh lemon juice

2 teaspoons honey

½ teaspoon salt

¼ teaspoon freshly ground
    black pepper

⅓ cup (75 ml) extra virgin olive oil

6 ounces (180 g) baby arugula

⅓ cup (10 g) fresh mint leaves, torn
    into pieces

2 large, ripe but firm white peaches,
    halved, pitted, and thinly sliced

8 thin slices prosciutto, about
    4 ounces (115 g)

¼ cup (30 g) shaved Parmesan cheese

24 green almonds, shelled, or ¼ cup
    (1 oz/30 g) sliced almonds,
    toasted (see page 41)

Whisk the lemon juice, honey, salt, and pepper together in a small bowl. Slowly add the olive oil in a steady stream, whisking constantly to emulsify.

Toss the arugula and half of the mint in a large bowl. Drizzle with half of the dressing and toss to combine.

Place a mound of arugula on each serving plate. Fan the slices of half a peach along one side of the arugula. Drape two slices of prosciutto around the other side of the arugula. Sprinkle each serving with some of the cheese and scatter 6 almonds over the peaches and prosciutto. Garnish with the remaining mint. Serve the remaining dressing on the side.

SERVES 4

Peaches and Almonds, Pierre Auguste Renoir, c. 1901

Mixed Greens with Roasted Beets, Feta, and Toasted Almonds

Nuts are a great addition to salads, adding flavor and substance. Here, toasted almonds join sweet beets, salty feta, and mixed greens. The fragrant pan juices from the roasted beets serve as a marinade for the cooling beets and are later added to the salad dressing. Prepare the beets up to one day in advance. Their flavor will improve the longer they marinate.

4 golden or red beets,
    about 1 pound (450 g)

⅓ cup (75 ml) extra virgin olive oil

1 teaspoon salt

2 tablespoons fresh lemon juice

1 tablespoon champagne or white
    balsamic vinegar

½ teaspoon freshly ground
    black pepper

6 cups (180 g) mixed greens
    (such as arugula, chicory, mizuna,
    and/or red oak lettuce)

½ cup (75 g) crumbled feta cheese

⅓ cup (1½ oz/45 g) raw almonds,
    toasted (see page 41) and
    coarsely chopped

¼ cup (7 g) fresh tarragon leaves,
    torn in half if large

Preheat the oven to 400°F (200°C).

Scrub the beets and trim the tips and tails to within 1 inch (2.5 cm). Place in a rimmed baking pan or small ovenproof pot with a lid. Pour the oil over the beets, turning to coat, and sprinkle with salt. Cover with aluminum foil or a lid and roast until the beets are just tender when pierced with a knife, 50 to 60 minutes. Transfer the beets to a cutting board and let cool to the touch, then slip off their skins.

Pour the pan juices into a medium bowl. Slice each beet into 6 or 8 wedges. Add to the pan juices and toss to coat. Proceed with the recipe now, or cover and refrigerate for up to 24 hours. Using a slotted spoon, transfer the beets to a plate. Add the lemon juice, vinegar, and black pepper to the pan juices. Whisk to combine.

Place the greens in a large serving bowl. Drizzle with half of the dressing and toss to combine. Scatter the beets, feta, and almonds over the greens. Drizzle with more dressing to taste. Garnish with tarragon.

SERVES 4

Provençal Tuna Salad with Almonds, Olives, and Capers in Lettuce Cups

Classic tuna salad gets a fresh treatment in this robust chopped salad full of flavors from the south of France. Olive oil and lemon replace mayonnaise, while celery is joined by almonds, olives, and capers. Serve in lettuce cups as a healthful appetizer, or spread on crostini or bruschetta.

Les Tres Riches Heures, Janvier, Limbourg Brothers, c. 1414

2 (6-oz/180-g) cans oil-packed tuna, drained

2 ribs celery, cut into ¼-inch (6-mm) dice

1 small red bell pepper, seeded and deveined, cut into ¼-inch (6-mm) dice

½ small red onion, finely chopped, about ½ cup (75 g)

¼ cup (1 oz/30g) pitted kalamata olives, sliced

¼ cup (1 oz/30 g) raw almonds, toasted (see page 41) and coarsely chopped

Juice of ½ lemon

2 tablespoons extra virgin olive oil, plus extra for drizzling

1 tablespoon capers, drained and rinsed

1 teaspoon salt, or to taste

1 teaspoon freshly ground black pepper

Dash of Tabasco sauce

½ cup (15 g) fresh flat-leaf parsley leaves, chopped

12 Boston lettuce leaves or large Little Gem leaves

Combine all of the ingredients except the parsley and lettuce in a large bowl. Toss to thoroughly combine. Taste and adjust the seasoning. Fold in the parsley.

Divide the lettuce leaves among individual salad plates or arrange together on a large serving platter. Divide the tuna mixture among the lettuce leaves. Drizzle with a little olive oil and serve.

Variation: Omit the lettuce leaves and spread the tuna salad on crostini or bruschetta.

MAKES 12 LETTUCE CUPS: SERVES 4 TO 6 AS A FIRST COURSE

Roasted Cauliflower with Dukkah

In Egyptian homes, dukkah is served as a meze, or appetizer, usually as a dip. Dukkah means "to pound" in Arabic, which aptly sums up the method for preparing this crumbly condiment. The blend of nuts and spices varies from family to family, but usually includes almonds, sesame, cumin, and coriander, which are toasted and ground together in a mortar. The recipe makes more than you will need here; cover and refrigerate the extra spice mix for up to one month and serve it as a meze by dipping toasted or grilled pita bread in olive oil, then in the dukkah.

1 large head cauliflower, cored and broken into bite-sized florets

2 tablespoons extra virgin olive oil, plus extra for drizzling

1 teaspoon salt

DUKKAH

¼ cup (1 oz/30 g) raw almonds

2 tablespoons sesame seeds

1 teaspoon coriander seeds

1 teaspoon cumin seeds

½ teaspoon fennel seeds

¼ teaspoon black peppercorns

¼ teaspoon red pepper flakes

½ teaspoon salt

Preheat the oven to 400°F (200°C). Toss the cauliflower with the 2 tablespoons olive oil and the salt in a large bowl. Spread on a rimmed baking sheet. Roast until tender and lightly golden brown, about 20 minutes.

While the cauliflower is roasting, make the dukkah: Heat a heavy, medium skillet over medium heat. Add the almonds and toast, stirring frequently, until lightly browned, about 2 minutes. Remove from the heat and pour the almonds onto a plate to cool. Add the sesame seeds to the same skillet and toast, stirring, until light golden brown, about 30 seconds. Pour the seeds onto the plate with the nuts. Add the coriander, cumin, fennel, and peppercorns to the skillet and toast, stirring, until fragrant, about 1 minute. Pour onto the same plate and let cool completely.

Transfer the nut mixture to a food processor or mortar. Add the pepper flakes and salt. Pulse or pound to a crumbly consistency. Do not overprocess.

Transfer the roasted cauliflower to a platter. Drizzle with a little olive oil. Sprinkle with 2 to 3 tablespoons of the dukkah and serve warm.

SERVES 4 AS A SIDE DISH

Brussels Sprouts with Bacon and Almonds

Sometimes Brussels sprouts need a little help. In this recipe, bacon, garlic, and almonds come to the rescue, transforming the humble vegetable into a side dish that even the most ardent sprout hater will enjoy. Don't forget the soy sauce; not only does it add saltiness, it also adds an addictive quality that will encourage second helpings. Select larger sprouts, which are easier to quarter. If using small sprouts, cut them in half.

6 ounces (180 g) thick-cut bacon, cut into ½-inch (12-mm) pieces

1 tablespoon extra virgin olive oil

1 clove garlic, minced

½ cup (2 oz/60 g) sliced almonds

2 pounds (900 g) large Brussels sprouts, trimmed and quartered

2 tablespoons soy sauce

Salt and freshly ground black pepper

Place the bacon in a large skillet and fry over medium heat until the fat renders and the bacon is crisp. Using a slotted spoon, transfer to a plate lined with a paper towel to drain.

Pour off all but 1 tablespoon bacon fat from the skillet. Add the olive oil, garlic, and almonds to the skillet. Sauté over medium heat until the garlic is fragrant, 1 minute. Add the Brussels sprouts and soy sauce. Cook, stirring frequently, until the sprouts are tender, 6 to 8 minutes. Stir in the bacon. Season with salt and pepper to taste. Serve warm.

SERVES 6 AS A SIDE DISH

Winter Kale and Quinoa Salad with Carrots and Raisins

This hearty winter side dish is brimming with good health and flavor. Earthy kale, red cabbage, and carrots are accompanied with protein-rich quinoa, toasted almonds, and sweet raisins. The result is a colorful, textured salad sparked with a citrus vinaigrette that promises to keep the doctor away. Before tossing the greens, it's essential to massage the kale leaves with lemon juice, oil, and salt just long enough to soften the sturdy leaves.

1 large bunch green curly kale, tough veins removed and leaves coarsely chopped

2 tablespoons fresh lemon juice

1 tablespoon extra virgin olive oil

Pinch of salt

VINAIGRETTE

2 tablespoons balsamic vinegar

2 tablespoons minced shallots

½ teaspoon freshly ground black pepper

½ teaspoon salt

¼ cup (60 ml) extra virgin olive oil

1 large carrot, peeled and shredded

1½ cups (120 g) thinly sliced red cabbage

½ cup (90 g) cooked quinoa

¼ cup (1 oz/30 g) sliced almonds

¼ cup (45 g) golden raisins

Place the kale in a large serving bowl. Add the lemon juice, oil, and salt. Massage the kale until it begins to soften, about 2 minutes. Set aside.

To make the vinaigrette: Whisk the vinegar, shallots, black pepper, and salt together in a small bowl. Slowly add the olive oil in a steady stream, whisking constantly to emulsify. Set aside.

Add the carrot, cabbage, quinoa, almonds, and raisins to the kale. Toss with half of the dressing, then add the remaining dressing to taste.

SERVES 4 TO 6 AS A FIRST COURSE

Green Beans with Almonds

Green beans amandine is a classic French preparation of blanched beans sautéed in butter. The minimal list of ingredients produces delicious results that pair the toasted flavor of pan-fried almonds with the astringent sweetness of fresh green beans. This recipe skips the blanching step, keeping the beans bright in color and crisp-tender. Green or yellow wax beans, or a combination of the two, may be used.

1 tablespoon unsalted butter

1 tablespoon extra virgin olive oil

¼ cup (1 oz/30 g) slivered almonds

1 pound (450 g) green beans, trimmed

1 clove garlic, minced

1 teaspoon salt

Melt the butter with the olive oil in a large skillet over medium heat. Add the almonds. Cook, stirring, until the almonds begin to turn golden brown. Using a slotted spoon, quickly transfer to a plate lined with a paper towel.

Add the beans to the skillet. Sauté until they turn bright green, about 3 minutes. Add the garlic and salt. Partially cover the pan and cook, stirring frequently, until the beans are crisp-tender, about 2 minutes longer. Transfer to a warmed serving bowl. Sprinkle with the reserved almonds. Serve warm.

SERVES 4 AS A SIDE DISH

ALMONDS AT HOME AND IN FINE DINING

The almond is an amazing ingredient with a seemingly unlimited number of uses in both home and professional kitchens. At home I love to use almonds in place of pine nuts in pestos, such as an arugula and almond pesto I toss with farfalle pasta and sprinkle with a little pecorino cheese. Because almonds and pine nuts both have a high fat content, they substitute for each other beautifully. At my restaurant, Niche, we use almonds to thicken a traditional white gazpacho, which we serve with a smoked Concord grape sorbet. It is amazing to find an ingredient that is delicious eaten alone, lightly roasted with just a little bit of sea salt and olive oil, but that can also be used in a complex dessert like an almond financier with rhubarb jam, pink peppercorn powder, and goat's milk sorbet. As a chef, I've found working with almonds to be truly magical, and I am fortunate that I get to celebrate them every day.

—Gerard Craft, chef, Niche, St. Louis

Roasted Acorn Squash Stuffed with Rice, Cranberries, and Almonds

Besides being a substantial side dish or a hearty vegetarian entrée, this sweet acorn squash, filled with an autumnal rice blend, looks beautiful on the holiday table. Partially cooking the squash before stuffing ensures that the flesh will be fully cooked and tender. Kabocha may be substituted for the acorn squash. Be sure to select squash with stems that are fresh and intact.

Still Life of Plums, Peaches, Almonds and Grapes, Willem van Aelst, 1650

2 acorn squash, halved vertically, seeds and membranes removed

Extra virgin olive oil, for coating and drizzling

Salt and freshly ground black pepper

1 tablespoon unsalted butter

½ cup (75 g) minced shallots

1 clove garlic, minced

1 teaspoon dried thyme

2 cups (285 g) cooked wild or brown rice

¼ cup (45 g) dried cranberries

¼ cup (1 oz/30 g) raw almonds, toasted (see page 41) and chopped

Minced fresh flat-leaf parsley, for garnish

Preheat the oven to 425°F (220°C).

Lightly coat the squash on all sides with olive oil. Lightly season the cut sides with salt and pepper. Place cut side down in a large baking dish. Roast until just fork-tender, 25 to 30 minutes. Reduce the oven temperature to 375°F (190°C).

Melt the butter in a medium saucepan over medium heat. Add the shallots and sauté until translucent, about 2 minutes. Add the garlic and thyme. Sauté until fragrant, 1 minute. Remove from the heat. Stir in the rice, cranberries, and almonds. Season to taste with salt and pepper.

Mound the rice into the centers of the squash. Drizzle with olive oil. Return to the oven and roast until rice begins to brown on top and the squash are very tender, about 30 minutes. Garnish with parsley and serve warm.

SERVES 4 AS A SUBSTANTIAL SIDE DISH, 2 AS A MAIN COURSE

Sautéed Spinach with Almonds, Chickpeas, and Lemon

Wilted spinach is dressed up with almonds and chickpeas in this colorful side dish inspired by the flavors of the Middle East. This easy recipe comes together in minutes. Don't be fooled by the quantity of spinach required. It will cook down to a surprisingly modest amount.

2 tablespoons extra virgin olive oil

½ cup (2 oz/60 g) slivered almonds

Pinch of salt, plus ½ teaspoon

1 onion, sliced crosswise

1 cup (185 g) canned chickpeas (garbanzo beans), drained, rinsed, and dried

2 cloves garlic, minced

1 teaspoon ground cumin

½ teaspoon ground coriander

½ teaspoon red pepper flakes

1 pound (450 g) spinach, stemmed

1 tablespoon fresh lemon juice

1 teaspoon finely grated lemon zest

Heat the olive oil in a large sauté pan over medium heat. Add the almonds and a pinch of salt. Sauté the almonds, stirring constantly, until golden brown, about 1 minute. Using a slotted spoon, transfer the nuts to a plate.

Add the onion to the same pan and sauté until softened and golden, 3 to 4 minutes. Add the chickpeas, garlic, cumin, coriander, and red pepper flakes. Sauté until fragrant, 1 minute. Add the spinach. Cover and cook until the spinach wilts, about 2 minutes. Remove from the heat and stir in the almonds, lemon juice, zest and the ½ teaspoon salt. Taste and adjust the seasoning. Serve warm.

SERVES 4

Zucchini Carpaccio with Toasted Almonds

Thinly sliced zucchini ribbons are julienned in this light and delicate Italian side dish adapted from a recipe shared by Jack Kreitzman, chef and owner of San Francisco's Jackson Fillmore Trattoria. The beauty is in the simplicity of this dish, so be sure to use zucchini at season's peak and the best-quality olive oil you can find.

2 medium-large zucchini, ends trimmed

3 tablespoons extra virgin olive oil

½ cup (2 oz/60 g) sliced almonds

½ teaspoon kosher salt, or to taste

Freshly ground black pepper

¼ cup (30 g) shaved pecorino romano cheese

3 tablespoons minced fresh flat-leaf parsley

Cut the zucchini lengthwise into ribbons ⅛ inch (3 mm) thick, using either a chef's knife or a mandoline. Stack the ribbons neatly and cut the stack into ¼-inch (6-mm) julienne. Set aside.

Heat 2 tablespoons of the olive oil in a medium skillet over medium heat. Add the almonds and toast, stirring constantly, until light brown, about 2 minutes. Sprinkle with salt to taste. Remove from the heat. Add the zucchini and toss until slightly wilted but still crisp, about 30 seconds. Add pepper to taste.

Crumble the cheese and sprinkle over the zucchini. Sprinkle with the parsley. Drizzle with the remaining 1 tablespoon olive oil and serve.

SERVES 4 AS A SIDE DISH

PASTA & GRAINS

Greek Orzo Salad with Zucchini, Tomato, Feta, and Almonds

Orzo, a rice-shaped pasta, is popular in Greek cuisine. It maintains its shape when cooked and is ideal in pasta salads, soups, and pilafs.

8 ounces (225 g) orzo pasta

1 tablespoon extra virgin olive oil, plus extra for brushing

1 tablespoon fresh lemon juice

1 teaspoon finely grated lemon zest

2 small zucchini, cut into disks ½ inch (12 mm) thick

Salt for sprinkling, plus 1 teaspoon

1 cup (180 g) cherry tomatoes, halved (quartered if large)

1 clove garlic, minced

½ cup (75 g) coarsely crumbled feta cheese

¼ cup (1 oz/30 g) sliced almonds

¼ cup (7 g) chopped fresh mint

¼ cup (7 g) chopped fresh flat-leaf parsley

1 teaspoon freshly ground black pepper

Bring a large pot of salted water to a rolling boil. Add the orzo and cook until al dente, about 9 minutes. Drain. Transfer to a large serving bowl and toss with 1 tablespoon olive oil, the lemon juice, and zest.

Preheat the broiler. Brush the zucchini slices with olive oil. Lightly season with salt. Place on a broiler pan and broil 2 inches (5 cm) from the heat source, turning once, until tender and light golden brown, 10 to 12 minutes.

Remove and let cool to the touch. Cut the slices in half and place them in the serving bowl. Add the tomatoes, garlic, feta, almonds, mint, parsley, 1 teaspoon salt, and pepper. Toss to combine. Taste and adjust the seasoning. Serve slightly warm or at room temperature.

SERVES 4 AS A LIGHT MAIN COURSE

Soba Noodles with Spicy Almond Butter Sauce

Soba, Japanese noodles made of buckwheat flour, are typically served in cold noodle salads or warm broth. Their hearty, satisfying flavor stands up well to spices and aromatics such as chile and garlic. Almonds replace peanuts in this popular preparation. Sriracha, a Thai hot sauce, can be found in most supermarkets.

ALMOND BUTTER SAUCE

¼ cup (60 g) almond butter (see page 54)

3 tablespoons fresh lime juice

1 tablespoons soy sauce

1 tablespoon light brown sugar

2 teaspoons hot sauce, such as Sriracha

2 teaspoons Asian sesame oil

1 small clove garlic, minced

NOODLES

8 ounces (225 g) soba noodles

4 green onions, white and green parts, thinly sliced

1 large carrot, peeled and cut into matchsticks

1 red jalapeño or serrano chile, seeded and minced

½ English cucumber, peeled, seeded, and cut into matchsticks

½ cup (20 g) chopped fresh cilantro

¼ cup (1 oz/30 g) slivered almonds

1 tablespoon sesame seeds, toasted (see page 68)

To make the sauce, whisk all the ingredients together in a small bowl; set aside.

Bring a large pot of salted water to a rolling boil over high heat. Add the noodles and cook, stirring occasionally, until al dente, about 5 minutes. Drain and rinse in cold water. Drain again and place in a large serving bowl.

Pour the sauce over the noodles. Add the green onions, carrot, chile, cucumber, cilantro, and almonds. Toss until all of the ingredients are coated. Sprinkle with sesame seeds and serve at room temperature.

SERVES 4

Toasted Pearl Couscous with Almonds and Harissa

Ptitim, also called Israeli couscous, was created as a rice substitute for Jewish immigrants from Arab and Muslim countries. The tiny pearls of pasta-like toasted wheat are significantly larger than semolina couscous and hold their shape while cooking. When browned in olive oil before being simmered in liquid, they take on a golden hue and add a warm, toasted flavor to any dish. Harissa, a Moroccan chile paste, adds spiciness to this side dish, which is lovely alongside grilled meats and fish. Harissa can be found in the international section of supermarkets, or you can substitute another hot sauce such as Sriracha.

3 tablespoons extra virgin olive oil, divided

2 cups (350 g) Israeli couscous

1¾ cups (425 ml) water or chicken stock

1 teaspoon salt

2 tablespoons fresh lime juice

2 teaspoons harissa paste or Sriracha sauce

½ teaspoon ground cumin

½ teaspoon freshly ground black pepper

¼ cup (10 g) chopped fresh cilantro

¼ cup (1 oz/30 g) sliced almonds

Heat 1 tablespoon of the oil in a medium sauté pan over medium heat. Add the couscous. Cook, stirring, until the couscous is light golden brown, about 2 minutes.

Carefully add the water or stock (it will sizzle when added to the skillet) and salt. Bring to a boil, then reduce the heat to low. Cover and simmer until all of the liquid is absorbed, 6 to 8 minutes.

Transfer the couscous to a large bowl and fluff it with a fork. Add 1 tablespoon of the olive oil, the lime juice, harissa, cumin, and pepper. Let cool slightly, then stir in the cilantro and almonds. Drizzle with the remaining 1 tablespoon olive oil and toss to combine. Serve warm or at room temperature.

SERVES 4 TO 6 AS A SIDE DISH

Almond and Saffron Rice Pilaf

Homemade rice pilaf is easy to make from scratch and a healthy alternative to packaged store-bought pilaf. Sautéing and steaming the rice in a rich stock creates an aromatic dish to complement any entrée. No wonder it's a staple throughout Asia and the Middle East.

3 cups (750 ml) chicken stock

¼ teaspoon saffron threads

2 tablespoons unsalted butter

½ cup (2 oz/60 g) slivered almonds

½ cup (60 g) chopped yellow onion

½ cup (105 g) whole-wheat
    orzo pasta

1½ cups (300 g) basmati rice

1 teaspoon kosher salt

Heat the stock in a small saucepan over medium heat. Add the saffron and remove from the heat.

Melt the butter in a medium saucepan over medium heat. Add the almonds and cook, stirring constantly, until golden. Using a slotted spoon, transfer the almonds to a plate lined with a paper towel.

Add the onion to the saucepan and cook over medium heat, stirring occasionally, until translucent, about 3 minutes. Add the orzo and sauté 1 minute. Add the rice and stir to coat. Add the saffron-infused stock and salt. Bring to a boil. Reduce the heat to low and cook, covered, until the rice is tender and the liquid is absorbed, about 15 minutes. Remove from the heat and let stand, covered, for 5 minutes.

Fluff the rice with a fork and stir in the almonds. Serve immediately.

SERVES 4 TO 6 AS A SIDE DISH

Farrotto with Almonds, Shiitake Mushrooms, and Balsamic-Glazed Radicchio

Farro replaces rice in this rustic dish inspired by Italian risotto. Farro is an ancient whole-wheat grain originating in the Mediterranean and Middle East. Its hearty, nutty flavor complements the earthy mushrooms, toasted almonds, and radicchio in this recipe. Balsamic vinegar, used to glaze the radicchio, reduces its bitterness and balances the farrotto.

2 tablespoons extra virgin olive oil, divided

¼ cup (45 g) minced shallots

8 ounces (225 g) shiitake mushrooms, stemmed and sliced ¼ inch (6 mm) thick

1 teaspoon salt, divided

1 clove garlic, minced

1 tablespoon minced fresh thyme, or 1 teaspoon dried thyme

1½ cups (300 g) farro

½ cup (125 ml) dry white wine

1½ cups (375 ml) chicken stock

1 small radicchio, cored and sliced

¼ cup (60 ml) balsamic vinegar

½ cup (2 oz/60 g) raw almonds, toasted (see page 41) and coarsely chopped

½ cup (60 g) grated Parmigiano-Reggiano cheese

Freshly ground black pepper

Minced fresh flat-leaf parsley, for garnish

Gathering Almond Blossoms, John William Waterhouse, 1916

(continued next page)

Heat 1 tablespoon of the oil in a large, heavy saucepan over medium heat. Add the shallot and cook, stirring, until softened, about 2 minutes. Add the mushrooms and ½ teaspoon of the salt. Sauté until the mushrooms begin to soften, about 2 minutes. Add the garlic and thyme. Continue to cook, stirring, until the mushrooms begin to release their juices, about 2 minutes. Add the farro and stir to coat. Add the wine and cook until the liquid is nearly evaporated. Add the stock. Bring to a boil, then reduce heat to low. Cover and simmer until the farro is tender and the liquid is absorbed, about 30 minutes.

While the farro is cooking, heat the remaining 1 tablespoon olive oil in a large skillet over medium-high heat. Add the radicchio and sauté for 1 minute. Add the balsamic vinegar and cook, stirring, until vinegar has thickened and coats the radicchio, about 1 minute. Remove from the heat and season with the remaining ½ teaspoon salt.

Stir in the radicchio, half of the almonds, half of the cheese, and season with freshly ground pepper. Taste and adjust the seasoning. Divide the farro among serving bowls. Sprinkle with the remaining almonds and the remaining cheese. Garnish with parsley. Serve immediately.

SERVES 4 TO 6 AS A SIDE DISH

Selling of Almond Oil, Tacuinum Sanitatis, c.1300

Linguine with Almonds and Garlic

Less is more in this simple Italian pasta dish, the epitome of comfort food. Requiring just a handful of humble ingredients and less than 30 minutes to prepare, it will transform a casual weeknight dinner into a feast. Instead of the usual bread crumbs, finely chopped almonds dress the garlicky linguine. The red pepper flakes add a little kick of heat.

1 pound (450 g) linguine pasta

¼ cup (60 ml) extra virgin olive oil

½ cup (2 oz/60 g) raw almonds, finely chopped

2 cloves garlic cloves, minced

½ teaspoon red pepper flakes

½ teaspoon salt

½ teaspoon freshly ground black pepper

½ cup (60 g) finely grated pecorino romano cheese

½ cup (20 g) chopped fresh flat-leaf parsley

Bring a large pot of salted water to a rolling boil. Add the linguine and cook until al dente, about 9 minutes. Drain, reserving 1 cup (250 ml) cooking water.

While the pasta is cooking, heat the olive oil in a large sauté pan over medium heat. Add the almonds and cook, stirring, until they begin to turn color, about 1 minute. Add the garlic and pepper flakes. Cook, stirring, until the almonds and garlic are golden, without letting them burn, about 30 seconds. Remove from the heat. Add the salt and pepper.

Add the cooked pasta to the sauté pan and toss to combine. If too dry, add a little of the reserved cooking water. Sprinkle with the cheese and parsley and toss again. Divide among serving plates. Serve warm.

SERVES 4

Nuts of all sorts are elegant "flavor-makers" in Lebanese cuisine. Without them, many of our dishes would feel underdressed, like a princess without her tiara. While the pistachio, the pine nut, and the walnut are all found on the Lebanese table, it is the almond that most captures my attention. Almond trees are abundant in Lebanon, and the nuts are eaten young and green in the spring. We often "fry" slivered almonds by sautéing them in butter until the nuts are a deep golden brown before sprinkling them with salt. It's nearly impossible not to eat some of them before they are put to use! I always seem to be shooing little hands away from the fried almond bowl while I'm cooking, so I always make extra. One of the favorite Lebanese dishes is *hushwe*, a rice pilaf redolent with cinnamon and lavished with a heap of golden slivered almonds. It's the kind of tiara we never leave behind.

—MAUREEN ABOOD, author of the blog
Rose Water & Orange Blossoms:
Modern Musings on Lebanese Cuisine

Bulgur Salad with Chickpeas, Pomegranate Seeds, and Almonds

Tabbouleh is a Syrian and Lebanese salad made with bulgur wheat and finely chopped herbs and vegetables. This recipe adds almonds, fresh chickpeas, and pomegranate seeds to the mix, resulting in a vibrant and substantial vegetarian main course or side dish.

Fresh chickpeas (garbanzo beans) resemble edamame and are pale green in color, with a papery pod that should be removed before eating. They are available fresh in markets in summer and may be found in the frozen section of some supermarkets. If desired, canned chickpeas may be substituted.

1½ cups (240 g) bulgur wheat

1¼ cups (310 ml) water

¼ cup (60 ml) fresh lemon juice

2 tablespoons extra virgin olive oil

1 teaspoon ground cumin

½ teaspoon ground coriander

1 teaspoon salt

1 teaspoon freshly ground
  black pepper

3 green onions, white and green
  parts, thinly sliced

1 red jalapeño or serrano chile,
  seeded and minced

1 large clove garlic, minced

1 pound (450 g) fresh chickpeas,
  shelled, or 1 cup (145 g)
  thawed frozen green chickpeas

⅓ cup (60 g) pomegranate seeds

¼ cup (1 oz/30 g) sliced almonds,
  lightly toasted (see page 41)

½ cup (15 g) packed fresh mint
  leaves, chopped

½ cup (15 g) packed fresh flat-leaf
  parsley leaves, chopped

Place the bulgur in a large heatproof bowl. Bring the water to a boil, then pour over the bulgur. Stir in the lemon juice, olive oil, cumin, coriander, salt, and pepper. Cover and let stand at room temperature until all of the liquid is absorbed and the bulgur is tender, about 20 minutes.

Fluff with a fork. Add all of the remaining ingredients except the mint and parsley and stir to combine. If the bulgur is too dry, add more olive oil or lemon juice. Taste and adjust the seasoning. Cover and refrigerate for up to 4 hours if not serving immediately.

Before serving, bring to room temperature if refrigerated. Add the mint and parsley and gently combine.

SERVES 4 TO 6 AS A SIDE DISH

Bucatini with Pesto Trapanese

Pesto trapanese originated in the Trapani harbor of Sicily. It's believed that Genoese sailors, passing through to Asia from Liguria, introduced their version of pesto genovese, inspiring the trapanese version, which adds almonds and cherry tomatoes. Bucatini is a thick spaghetti-shaped pasta with a hole running through the center. Spaghetti may be substituted for the bucatini.

PESTO

½ cup (2 oz/60 g) raw almonds, lightly toasted (see page 41)

1 cup (30 g) fresh basil leaves, lightly packed

2 cloves garlic

½ teaspoon sea salt

¼ teaspoon red pepper flakes

1 pound (450 g) cherry tomatoes

½ cup (125 ml) extra virgin olive oil

1 pound (450 g) bucatini pasta

½ cup (60 g) finely grated pecorino romano cheese

To make the pesto, pulse the almonds in a food processor to the size of rice grains. Transfer to a bowl.

Add the basil, garlic, salt, and pepper flakes to the food processor. Pulse until finely chopped. Return the almonds to the food processor. Add the tomatoes. With the machine running, add the oil in a steady stream to emulsify and form a thick purée. Taste and adjust the seasoning.

Bring a large pot of salted water to a rolling boil. Add the pasta and cook until al dente, about 9 minutes. Drain.

Pour the pesto into a large bowl. Add the pasta and toss to coat. Add the cheese and toss again. Serve immediately.

SERVES 4 AS A LIGHT MAIN COURSE

LAND & SEA

Almond-Crusted Pork Chops with Sweet-and-Sour Apricot Glaze

Apricot preserves, soy sauce, mustard, and fresh ginger come together in an East-meets-West sweet-and-sour sauce that serves as both a tenderizing marinade and a finishing sauce. Crushed almonds coat the pork, adhering to the sticky marinade and creating a crisp and nutty crust.

MARINADE

2 cloves garlic, minced

½ cup (145 g) apricot preserves

¼ cup (125 ml) soy sauce

2 tablespoons fresh lime juice

1 tablespoon extra virgin olive oil

1 tablespoon Dijon mustard

1 tablespoon finely grated peeled ginger with juice

1 teaspoon ground cumin

1 teaspoon ground cardamom

4 bone-in pork chops, 1 inch (2.5 cm) thick

1 cup (4 oz/115 g) raw almonds, finely chopped

1 tablespoon extra virgin olive oil

To make the marinade, whisk all the ingredients together in a bowl. Transfer half of the marinade to a small bowl and reserve for the sauce.

Place the pork in a shallow dish. Pour the remaining marinade over the pork and turn to coat. Cover and refrigerate for at least 2 hours or up to 4 hours. Remove from refrigerator 30 minutes before cooking.

Preheat the oven to 375°F (190°C). Pour the almonds onto a rimmed baking sheet. Using tongs, transfer pork to the baking sheet. Discard the marinade. Turn the pork to coat it on all sides with the almonds.

Heat the oil in a large ovenproof skillet over medium-high heat. Add the pork in one layer and brown on all sides, about 5 minutes. Transfer the skillet to the oven and bake until the pork is firm to the touch and pale pink in the center, 10 to 12 minutes.

Transfer the pork to a warmed serving platter. Add the reserved marinade to the pan. Stir over medium heat to scrape up the browned bits on the bottom of the pan. Pour over the pork. Serve immediately.

SERVES 4

Pulled Pork with Red Mole

Legend has it that when a group of nuns in a Puebla, Mexico, convent were in a cooking panic due to the unexpected arrival of an archbishop, they created a mole sauce by using every ingredient at their disposal, including nuts, chocolate, dried fruit, chiles, and spices. Today, there are many versions of mole sauce, with the most common being mole poblano, a red or brown sauce served with meat. This recipe, which includes chiles, tomatoes, chocolate, and almond butter, yields a deeply flavorful sauce with a kick of smoky heat. It's also cook-friendly and takes less than an hour to prepare. Any leftover mole may be stored in the refrigerator for up to 3 days or frozen for up to 3 months. Serve with poultry, meat, eggs, or as a sauce for enchiladas or tamales.

PORK

3 pounds (1.5 kg) boneless pork shoulder (butt), cut into 3-inch (7.5-mm) chunks

Salt and freshly ground black pepper

1 tablespoon ground cumin

1 tablespoon ancho chile powder

2 tablespoons olive oil

1 cup (250 ml) Mexican beer

1 cup (250 ml) fresh orange juice

1 yellow onion, cut into wedges

3 cloves garlic

MOLE

2 tablespoons olive oil

1 yellow onion, chopped

2 cloves garlic, minced

2 teaspoons ancho chile powder

2 teaspoons pasilla chile powder

2 teaspoons ground cumin

1 teaspoon ground coriander

½ teaspoon cayenne pepper

¼ teaspoon ground cinnamon

⅛ teaspoon ground cloves

1 (15-oz/430-g) can plum tomatoes, drained and coarsely chopped

1 cup (250 ml) chicken stock

2 tablespoons raisins

1½ tablespoons almond butter (see page 54)

1 tablespoon unsweetened cocoa powder

1 teaspoon salt, or to taste

ACCOMPANIMENTS

Warm corn tortillas

Chopped yellow onion

Chopped jalapeño chile

Diced avocado

Fresh cilantro sprigs

(continued next page)

To prepare the pork, preheat the oven to 300°F (150°C). Pat the pork dry and season with salt and pepper. Sprinkle with the cumin and chili powder.

Heat the oil in a large Dutch oven or ovenproof pot with a lid. Add the pork in batches, without over-crowding, and brown on all sides. Using a slotted spoon, transfer to a plate. Drain off the fat in the pot.

Add the beer to the pot and stir over medium heat to scrape up the browned bits from the bottom of the pot. Add the orange juice and return the pork to the pot. Add the onion and garlic. Cover and bake in the oven, stirring once or twice, until the meat is very tender, about 3 hours.

While the pork is cooking, prepare the mole. Heat the oil in a medium sauté pan over medium heat. Add the onion and sauté until golden brown, about 5 minutes. Add the garlic, chile powders, cumin, coriander, cayenne, cinnamon, and cloves. Sauté until fragrant, about 1 minute. Add all the remaining mole ingredients and reduce the heat to low. Simmer uncovered, stirring occasionally, over low heat for 20 minutes. Carefully transfer to a food processor and purée until smooth. Taste and adjust the seasoning.

Using a slotted spoon, transfer the pork to a platter. Discard the onion and garlic. Boil the braising liquid until reduced by half. While the liquid is reducing, preheat the broiler. Shred the pork and discard any fat or gristle. Arrange the meat in one layer in a baking dish. Spoon the reduced braising liquid over the pork. Place the pork under the broiler 2 inches (5 cm) from the heat source. Broil until the meat begins to caramelize and crisp, about 2 minutes.

To serve, place some of the pork in the center of a tortilla. Spoon a little mole sauce over the pork. Sprinkle with onion, jalapeño, avocado, and cilantro, and roll up to eat by hand.

SERVES 4 TO 6

Since Colonial days, almonds have been an Old World import to Mexico. Today, we find them in local markets, imported from California. In Mexico, we toast them on the *comal* or in a dry skillet to bring out their essential flavor. Almonds are a key ingredient in chocolate, Mexico's ritual drink, and in several versions of mole, the classic sauce. In fact, almonds are featured in each of the four meals we consume every day.

For *desayuno*, a light, organic, often liquid breakfast, almonds are used in *licuados*, the Mexican version of smoothies, especially *platanadas*, made with bananas, milk, honey, almonds, and Mexican vanilla. To make the chocolate drink *almendrado*, toasted peeled cacao beans, almonds, sugar, and cinnamon are stone ground and then mixed with hot water or milk and whipped into a frothy beverage that is consumed almost daily in Oaxaca.

For *almuerzo*, a heartier meal that is consumed midmorning, almonds are one of the twenty-plus ingredients used in *mole coloradito* to make *enchiladas oaxaqueñas*. Fresh corn tortillas are bathed in mole sauce, then covered with onion slices, fresh cheese, and parsley, often accompanied by eggs, beef, or pork.

Our main meal of the day is *comida*, which often features several important main dishes highlighting the flavor and texture of almonds. *Chiles rellenos de picadillo* are roasted and peeled chiles (in Oaxaca we use *chiles de agua, chiles poblanos, chiles jalapeños*, or the famous regional smoked *chiles pasillas oaxaqueño*) stuffed with a well-seasoned *picadillo*. This is a shredded-meat mixture with onions, tomatoes, and the Spanish/Moorish-influenced ingredients almonds, olives, and capers. The battered and fried chiles are served in a tomato *caldillo*, or light broth. A special version of this dish is made for Independence Day: *chiles en nogada*, which adds fruit to the filling and is covered in walnut sauce and topped with pomegranate seeds.

A popular Colonial stew is *estofado almendrado*. Made with a base of almonds, the smooth reddish or green sauce is served over chicken or beef tongue and garnished with pickled *chiles serranos*, olives, and capers.

A dish served at the most important occasions is the revered *mole negro*, in which almonds play an essential role. A mixture of many ingredients that are first toasted, roasted, or fried to bring out their flavors and then ground to a smooth sauce, *mole negro* is often served over turkey. This mole can be made from scratch or from pastes found in the markets. The pastes are reconstituted with tomatoes and tomatillos and the broth of whatever meat they are served with. *Mole negro* is always served and eaten with tortillas.

The evening meal is a light one called *cena. Sopa de almendra* is an almond soup made with nuts that have been blanched, peeled, and blended to a milky white puree, with chunks of chicken, eggs and carrots. The simplest of *cenas* is often a cup of hot chocolate *almendrado* with *pan dulce* or *churros*.

During *Dia de los Muertos* we adorn our altars with marzipan figures of fruits and vegetables, and almonds are used in many of the traditional desserts and pastries, such as coconut-almond flan. As an imported ingredient in the mestizo kitchen, almonds have found a prominent place in our diet and continue to rise in popularity as more people acknowledge their health benefits as well.

—SUSANA TRILLING, cooking instructor and author of *Seasons of My Heart: A Culinary Journey Through Oaxaca, Mexico,* and *My Search for the Seventh Mole*

Wine-Braised Chicken with Saffron and Almonds

In this Spanish stew, chicken breasts simmer in a rich wine and lemon broth thickened with almonds, garlic, and saffron. Be sure that the chicken is not completely submerged in the stock while braising to ensure that the skin remains intact.

¼ cup (60 ml) extra virgin olive oil

6 large cloves garlic

½ cup (2 oz/60 g) blanched almonds

½ teaspoon saffron threads

1 teaspoon kosher salt, plus extra for seasoning

½ teaspoon freshly ground black pepper, plus extra for seasoning

4 (8-oz/225-g) boneless chicken breast halves with skin

1 large yellow onion, chopped

1 lemon, scrubbed, cut into quarters, and seeded

2 cups (500 ml) chicken stock

½ cup (125 ml) dry white wine

1 bay leaf

1 tablespoon minced fresh thyme

Steamed rice, for serving

Preheat the oven to 375°F (190°C).

Heat the olive oil in a large skillet over medium heat. Add the garlic and almonds and fry, stirring frequently, until golden brown, about 2 minutes. Remove the skillet from the heat. Using a slotted spoon, transfer the almonds and garlic to a plate and let cool to the touch. Reserve the oil in the pan, and when cool, separate the garlic from the almonds.

In a mortar or a spice grinder, grind or pulse the saffron with the 1 teaspoon salt and the ½ teaspoon black pepper. Add the garlic, half of the almonds, and 1 tablespoon of the reserved cooking oil. Grind or process until a smooth paste forms.

Season the chicken all over with salt and pepper. Heat the same skillet with the reserved oil over medium-high heat. Place the chicken in the skillet, skin side down. Cook, turning once, until golden brown, 5 to 6 minutes. Place the chicken in one layer, skin side up, in a large casserole or baking dish.

Reduce the heat to medium. Add the onion and lemon to the skillet and sauté until the onion is golden, 5 to 6 minutes. Add the chicken stock, wine, bay leaf, and thyme. Bring to a simmer. Add the garlic paste and whisk until

Still Life with Pears, Lemons and Almonds, Georges Braque, 1927

smooth. Pour the sauce over the chicken. The chicken should not be completely submerged in the sauce. Cover with a lid or aluminum foil.

Transfer to the oven. Braise until the chicken is nearly cooked through, about 20 minutes. Remove the lid and continue to cook until the chicken is opaque throughout, 10 to 15 minutes. Remove from the oven and discard the lemon and bay leaf.

Coarsely chop the remaining almonds. Serve the chicken over rice, with the sauce ladled over. Garnish with the chopped almonds.

SERVES 4 TO 5

ALMONDS IN SPANISH CUISINE

The almond tree (*almendra*) was introduced to Spain and Portugal by the Moors, who popularized the use of the nut in cooking. Legend has it that a Moorish prince married a blond Northern beauty who pined for snow. To make her happy, the prince planted groves of almond trees, which blossomed white each year. Almonds are widely grown in Catalonia, Andalusia, Valencia, and the Balearic Islands. The harvest starts at the end of August. The fruit is shaken onto canvas sheets, the tough green skin is cut away, and the nuts are dried in the sun before being roasted or blanched.

There are two kinds of almonds cultivated in Spain, the slender oval-shaped Largueta, similar to those grown in California (brought there by Spanish colonizers), and the Marcona, called the queen of almonds, which is rounder, fatter, and unique to Spain.

Almonds are a key component in *gazpacho blanco*, a refreshing summer soup of ground almonds blended with grapes and garlic. They are also essential to two classic sauces of Catalonia: *romesco*, which is traditionally served with shellfish, and *picada*, a mixture of nuts, garlic, bread, and spices used to thicken sauces for *albondigas* (meatballs), pork, and chicken. Almonds are a mainstay in desserts and sweets, such as the *torta di Santiago* and *turrón*, a white nougat made from almonds and honey, traditionally served as a Christmas treat in Spain.

—Joyce Goldstein, chef, and author of
Tapas: Sensational Small Plates from Spain
and *Savoring Spain and Portugal*

ALMONDS IN INDIAN CUISINE

Almonds were introduced into India by the Moghuls in the sixteenth century, and today they are an important part of North Indian cuisine, which is recognized around the world as Mughlai food. Finely ground almonds—almond meal, also called almond flour—are used in marinades for meat dishes and stirred into curries as a thickener. Almond meal is also made into desserts as well as a sweet resembling marzipan. Almonds are not toasted in Indian recipes, but rather, often accompanied by raisins, are sautéed in butter or ghee and sprinkled on top of savory as well as sweet dishes as a garnish. In winter, a few almonds, soaked overnight in milk, drained, and served with a spoonful of honey at breakfast, are believed to strengthen the immune system.

—SUNEETA VASWANI, cooking instructor and author of *Easy Indian Cooking* and *The Complete Book of Indian Cooking*

Mughlai Chicken Biryani

Biryani comes with a pedigree, as it was originally served to India's Mughal emperors. Over time, it has evolved and been adopted in Southeast Asia and the Middle East, with numerous variations in spice and ingredients. Traditionally, biryani combines rice with a meat or vegetable curry thickened with an aromatic paste of almonds and garlic. Each component is cooked separately to optimize flavor before being layered in one dish. Note: Whole spices add to the aroma and flavor of the finished dish, but they should not be eaten.

Market Scene at Kand-i-Badam, Weighing and Transport of Almonds from the *Baburnama*, Sur Das, c. 1598

RICE

2 cups (420 g) basmati rice

1 (2-inch/5-cm) cinnamon stick

1 teaspoon salt

ALMOND-SPICE MIXTURE

½ cup (2 oz/60 g) blanched almonds

2 large cloves garlic

1 tablespoon grated ginger
  with juice

3 tablespoons canola oil, divided

8 black peppercorns

4 whole cloves

3 green cardamom pods

1 (2-inch/5-cm) cinnamon stick

1 bay leaf

2 large yellow onions, chopped

1 red jalapeño or Fresno chile,
  seeded and minced

2 teaspoons ground coriander

2 teaspoons ground cumin

1 teaspoon sweet Hungarian
  paprika

½ teaspoon ground turmeric

2 pounds (900 g) boneless chicken
  thighs, cut into 2-inch (5-cm)
  pieces

1 cup (250 ml) chicken stock

½ cup (125 g) whole-milk yogurt

¼ cup (60 ml) fresh lemon juice

2 teaspoons salt

½ cup (20 g) minced fresh cilantro,
  plus extra for garnish

Extra virgin olive oil for drizzling

(continued next page)

To make the rice, rinse it in a fine-mesh sieve. Transfer to a heavy, medium saucepan. Add water to cover by 3 inches (7.5 cm). Add the cinnamon stick and salt. Bring to a boil, then reduce the heat and simmer, uncovered, until the rice is al dente, 8 to 10 minutes (it will continue to cook when baked). Drain and set aside.

To make the almond-spice mixture, combine the almonds, garlic, ginger, and 1 tablespoon of the canola oil in a food processor or a mortar. Pulse or grind to a paste. Set aside.

Heat the remaining 2 tablespoons canola oil in a large sauté pan or Dutch oven over medium heat. Add the peppercorns, cloves, cardamom, cinnamon stick, and bay leaf. Sauté until fragrant, 1 minute. Add the onions. Sauté until the onions are translucent, about 3 minutes. Add the almond paste and sauté until fragrant and golden, 2 minutes. Stir in the chile, coriander, cumin, paprika, and turmeric. Sauté to release the flavors of the spices, 2 to 3 minutes.

Add the chicken. Cook, turning to brown the chicken on all sides and coat with the spices, 3 to 4 minutes. Add the chicken stock, yogurt, lemon juice, and salt. Bring to a boil, then reduce the heat to a simmer. Cover and cook over medium-low heat until the chicken is opaque throughout, about 20 minutes. Stir in the ½ cup (20 g) cilantro.

Preheat the oven to 350°F (180°C). Spoon one-third of the rice into the bottom of an oiled 9 by 13-inch (23 by 33-cm) baking dish or casserole. Spoon half of the chicken over the rice and top the chicken with one-third of the rice. Spoon the remainder of the chicken over the rice and top with the remaining rice. Drizzle with olive oil. Cover tightly with aluminum foil or a lid. Bake in the oven for 30 minutes or until the rice is tender. Serve garnished with cilantro.

SERVES 6 TO 8

Crispy Oven-Fried Chicken

Ground almonds, grated cheese, and bread crumbs create a crisp and tasty coating for chicken in this healthful preparation—a winner for any picnic. Feel free to use drumsticks, breasts, or thighs for this recipe and adjust the cooking time accordingly.

½ cup (2 oz/60 g) finely ground
   blanched almonds

½ cup (60 g) panko
   (Japanese bread crumbs)

½ cup (60 g) finely grated Asiago
   or Parmesan cheese

2 teaspoons salt

1 teaspoon freshly ground
   black pepper

2 pounds (900 g) boneless chicken
   thighs or breast halves,
   or 8 drumsticks

Extra virgin olive oil, for brushing

Olive oil spray

Preheat the oven to 400°F (200°C). Place a wire rack on a rimmed baking sheet or use a broiler pan. Lightly oil the rack or pan.

Combine the almonds, panko, cheese, salt, and pepper in a large bowl. Whisk to blend. Lightly brush the chicken pieces with olive oil. Add to bowl one piece at a time, turning to coat thoroughly and arrange on the wire rack or pan. Lightly spray with oil.

Bake in the oven until golden brown on the outside and opaque throughout, 25 to 35 minutes for boneless thighs or breasts, 45 to 50 minutes for drumsticks. The chicken is done when juices run clear when thickest part of the chicken is pierced with the tip of a knife.

SERVES 4

Almond- and Mint-Crusted Lamb Chops

The classic pairing of lamb and mint takes a rustic turn in this easy preparation.
The mustard and egg coating holds a fragrant crust of mint, garlic, and almonds in
place while the meat is pan-seared.

½ cup (2 oz/60 g) raw almonds, finely chopped

1 large clove garlic, minced

1 tablespoon minced fresh mint

2 tablespoons extra virgin olive oil, plus extra for drizzling

1 tablespoon Dijon mustard

1 large egg yolk

8 lamb loin chops, 1 inch (2.5 cm) thick, about 2 pounds (900 g)

Salt and freshly ground black pepper

Chopped fresh mint, for garnish

Preheat the oven to 400°F (200°C).

Mix the almonds, garlic, and minced mint together in a wide, shallow bowl. Whisk 1 tablespoon of the olive oil, the mustard, and egg yolk together in a small bowl.

Season the lamb with salt and pepper. Brush the lamb chops with the mustard mixture and sprinkle with salt and pepper. Dredge the chops in the almond mixture to coat both sides evenly.

Heat an ovenproof skillet over medium-high heat. Add the remaining 1 tablespoon olive oil. Brown the lamb, turning once, about 3 minutes per side.

Transfer the skillet to the oven and cook until a meat thermometer inserted in the center of a chop registers 130°F (54°C) for medium-rare, 8 to 10 minutes. Remove from the oven. Tent with aluminum foil and let rest for 10 minutes.

To serve, drizzle with olive oil and garnish with chopped mint.

SERVES 4 TO 8 (1 OR 2 CHOPS PER PERSON)

Lamb Tagine with Apricots, Almonds, and Honey

Mrouzia is a Moroccan celebratory stew enriched with butter and sweetened with fruit and honey, prepared in the days following Eid al-Kebir, the Festival of Sacrifice. This recipe is a lighter and slightly more savory version, with olive oil substituting for butter, and carrot and tomato adding brightness and acidity. The dish is best started a day in advance of serving to allow the spice-rubbed meat to marinate overnight.

SPICE RUB

1 tablespoon sweet Hungarian paprika

2 teaspoons salt

1 teaspoon ground cumin

1 teaspoon ground coriander

1 teaspoon freshly ground
    black pepper

½ teaspoon ground cinnamon

½ teaspoon ground ginger

½ teaspoon ground cardamom

¼ teaspoon ground nutmeg

¼ teaspoon ground cloves

¼ teaspoon cayenne pepper

3 pounds (1.5 kg) boneless lamb leg
    or shoulder, trimmed of excess
    fat and cut into chunks 1½-inch
    (4-cm) thick

4 tablespoons (60 ml) olive oil,
    divided

1 large yellow onion, chopped

4 cloves garlic, minced

3 to 4 cups (750 ml–1 l) chicken stock

¼ cup (60 g) tomato paste

1 teaspoon salt

2 large carrots, peeled and cut into
    slices ¼ inch (6 mm) thick

1 cup (4 oz/115 g) blanched almonds

1 cup (180 g) dried apricots,
    coarsely chopped

1 tablespoon honey, or to taste

Couscous, for serving

(continued next page)

To make the spice rub, combine all the ingredients in a small bowl and stir to blend.

Pat the lamb dry with paper towels and place in a large bowl. Toss with 2 tablespoons of the olive oil and add the spice rub, mixing to coat thoroughly. Cover and refrigerate for at least 4 hours or up to 24 hours. Remove from the refrigerator 30 minutes before cooking.

Preheat the oven to 300°F (150°C).

Heat 1 tablespoon of the olive oil over medium-high heat in a Dutch oven or large ovenproof pot with a lid. In batches, add the lamb in one layer without over-crowding. Brown on all sides. Using a slotted spoon, transfer to a plate.

Drain off all the fat from the pot. Add the remaining 1 tablespoon olive oil, the onion, and garlic. Sauté until the onion is translucent, about 3 minutes. Add 3 cups (750 ml) chicken stock, the tomato paste, and salt. Return the lamb with any collected juices to the pot. (The meat should be just submerged in the stock. Add more stock, if necessary, to cover.) Bring to a boil, then reduce the heat to a simmer. Cover and transfer to the oven. Cook, stirring occasionally, until the lamb is very tender, about 2 hours.

Almond Trees and Ruins, Sicily, John Peter Russell, c.1887

Remove from the oven and transfer to the stovetop. Using a slotted spoon, transfer the meat to a bowl. Boil the stock over medium-high heat until reduced by one-third and slightly thickened, skimming the fat from the top. Add the carrots, almonds, and apricots. Return the lamb to the stock. Simmer, partially covered, 30 minutes. Stir in the honey. Taste and adjust the seasoning. Serve hot, spooned over couscous.

SERVES 6 TO 8

Stir-Fried Beef and Broccoli with Almonds

Three is not a crowd when almonds join the classic beef and broccoli pairing in this Asian stir-fry. If you don't have a wok, use a large sauté pan. Be sure to have all of your ingredients ready, because this dish comes together quickly. Serve with rice.

MARINADE

2 tablespoons soy sauce

1 tablespoon Chinese rice wine or dry sherry

1 tablespoon sweet chile sauce

1 teaspoon cornstarch

1½ pounds (675 g) beef sirloin, sliced ½ inch (12 mm) thick against the grain

SAUCE

¼ cup (60 ml) soy sauce

2 tablespoons sweet chile sauce

2 tablespoons fresh lime juice

1 tablespoon Asian sesame oil

1 tablespoon brown sugar

1 teaspoon cornstarch

2 tablespoons canola or peanut oil, divided

1 small yellow onion, halved lengthwise and thinly sliced crosswise

2 cloves garlic, chopped

1 tablespoon finely grated fresh ginger

1 pound (450 g) broccoli, cut into bite-sized florets

¼ cup (1 oz/30 g) sliced almonds, toasted (see page 41)

Steamed rice, for serving

(continued next page)

ALMONDS IN CHINESE COOKING

Almonds are thought to have originated in China and Central Asia. Historically, they were used in Asia for cooking and in traditional Chinese medicine, which prescribes them for treating respiratory diseases as well as for keeping one's skin supple and glowing.

Considered both a healthful food and a symbol of beauty, almonds are used predominantly in making sweet drinks and desserts in Chinese cooking. For centuries, these nuts have been ground and simmered with rock sugar to make a sweet drink called almond tea. With the immigration of Chinese to America in the mid-1800s, the trademark Chinese-American dessert of almond cookies was invented. Found in most Chinese bakeries, the almond cookie is a prized sweet during Chinese New Year, when it symbolizes gold coins and represents good fortune for the year ahead.

—FARINA WONG KINGSLEY,
cooking instructor and author of
Meals in Minutes: Everyday Asian
and the blog *Farina's Asian Pantry*

To make the marinade, combine all the ingredients in a small bowl and whisk until smooth. Place the beef in a large bowl and pour the marinade over. Toss to thoroughly coat. Let stand at room temperature for 30 minutes.

To make the sauce, whisk the soy sauce, chile sauce, lime juice, sesame oil, brown sugar, and cornstarch together in a small bowl. Set aside.

Heat a wok or large sauté pan over high heat. Add 1 tablespoon of the oil and swirl to coat the bottom. When the oil is shimmering, carefully add the beef in batches without overcrowding. Brown on both sides, turning once, 3 to 4 minutes. Using a slotted spoon, transfer to a plate.

Add the remaining 1 tablespoon oil to the skillet. Add the onion, garlic, and ginger. Stir-fry until fragrant, 1 minute. Add the broccoli florets and stir-fry for 1 minute. Add the sauce. Stir-fry until the broccoli is crisp-tender, about 3 minutes. Return the beef and any collected juices to the pan. Cook briefly to heat through. Stir in the almonds. Serve with rice.

SERVES 4

Blossoming Almond Branch in a Glass with a Book, Vincent van Gogh, 1888

Spanish Meatballs in Onion and Almond Sauce

Who doesn't love a good meatball? It seems that every culture has a version of homey, comforting meatballs. In Spain, albondigas are served in a soup or wine sauce thickened with a paste of fried almonds, garlic, and bread called picada. This recipe keeps the filling to a minimum with just a little panko and egg, resulting in light but meaty morsels. Veal may be substituted for the beef.

MEATBALLS

1 pound (450 g) ground pork

1 pound (450 g) ground lean beef

1 cup (145 g) finely chopped
    yellow onion

3 cloves garlic, minced

1 large egg, lightly beaten

¼ cup (10 g) minced fresh
    flat-leaf parsley

¼ cup (1 oz/30 g) panko
    (Japanese bread crumbs)

2 teaspoons sweet Hungarian paprika

2 teaspoons salt

1 teaspoon ground cumin

1 teaspoon freshly ground
    black pepper

½ teaspoon ground cinnamon

½ teaspoon cayenne pepper

PICADA

1 tablespoon extra virgin olive oil

1 large slice rustic bread, ½ inch
    (12 mm) thick, torn into
    small pieces

⅓ cup (1½ oz/45 g) blanched
    almonds

2 large cloves garlic

Pinch of saffron threads

½ teaspoon salt

½ teaspoon freshly ground
    black pepper

¼ cup (60 ml) olive oil

½ cup (75 g) chopped yellow onion

1 cup (250 ml) chicken stock

½ cup (125 ml) dry white wine

(continued next page)

To make the meatballs, place all of the ingredients in a large bowl. Using your hands, combine without over-mixing. Using a light hand, form into balls 1½ inches (4 cm) in diameter and place on a plate. Cover with plastic wrap and refrigerate for at least 1 hour or up to 4 hours.

To make the picada, heat the olive oil in a large, heavy skillet over medium heat. Add the bread, almonds, and garlic. Fry, stirring frequently, until golden brown. Remove from the heat. Transfer to a mortar or food processor. Add the saffron, salt, and pepper. Grind to a paste and set aside. Wipe the skillet clean.

To cook the meatballs, increase the heat to medium-high and add the olive oil to the same skillet. Add the meatballs in batches without overcrowding. Cook, turning once, until browned, about 5 minutes. Using a slotted spoon, transfer to a plate lined with a paper towel. (The meatballs will not be cooked through at this point. They will continue to cook in the sauce.)

Drain off all but 1 tablespoon of the fat in the skillet. Return to medium heat and add the onion. Sauté until the onion is translucent, about 3 minutes. Add the stock and wine. Bring to a boil over high heat, then reduce heat to medium. Whisk in the picada. Add the meatballs to the skillet. Cover and cook until the meatballs are cooked through, 15 to 20 minutes.

SERVES 4 TO 6

Roasted Sea Bass with Orange, Olive, and Almond Gremolata

Thick white sea bass fillets are jazzed up with citrusy gremolata in this simple recipe. Gremolata is an Italian herbal condiment usually made with parsley, lemon zest, and garlic, though other leafy herbs may be used, as well as nuts and olives. This recipe, inspired by the flavors of Sicily, substitutes orange for lemon and adds briny green olives and almonds to the mix.

GREMOLATA

1 cup (145 g) green olives, such as Castelvetrano, pitted and coarsely chopped

½ cup (20 g) minced fresh flat-leaf parsley

¼ cup (1 oz/30 g) raw almonds, toasted (see page 41) and chopped

1 clove garlic, minced

1 tablespoon extra virgin olive oil

1 tablespoon fresh orange juice

2 teaspoons finely grated orange zest

½ teaspoon freshly ground black pepper

Salt to taste

4 (6- to 8-oz/180- to 225 g) sea bass fillets, 1 inch (2.5 cm) thick

Extra virgin olive oil for drizzling

Salt and freshly ground black pepper

1 tablespoon fresh orange juice

Preheat the oven to 475°F (245°C).

To make the gremolata, combine all of the ingredients in a small bowl and toss to combine.

Arrange the fish in a baking dish. Drizzle with olive oil and turn to coat. Season with salt and pepper.

Roast in the oven until opaque throughout, 12 to 15 minutes. Remove from the oven and drizzle with the orange juice. Sprinkle with the gremolata and serve.

SERVES 4

Catalan Fish Stew with Chorizo, Fennel, and Almond Picada

In Catalonia, fish stew is an everyday meal prepared with a bounty of seafood plucked from the waters along Spain's northeastern coast. Shellfish and firm-fleshed fish simmer in an aromatic tomato broth infused with saffron and fennel and spiced with chorizo. Picada, a potent paste made of finely ground almonds, garlic, and parsley, is stirred into the broth at the end to thicken the stock. Serve with crusty bread.

PICADA

½ cup (2 oz/60 g) raw almonds

2 cloves garlic

2 tablespoons extra virgin olive oil

2 tablespoons chopped fresh flat-leaf parsley

½ teaspoon freshly ground black pepper

¼ teaspoon salt

1 tablespoon extra virgin olive oil

12 ounces (340 g) Spanish chorizo sausage, sliced ¾ inch (2 cm) thick

1 yellow onion, chopped

1 fennel bulb, trimmed, halved lengthwise, and thinly sliced

2 cloves garlic, chopped

1 teaspoon sweet Hungarian paprika

1 teaspoon dried thyme

½ teaspoon fennel seeds

½ teaspoon saffron threads

1 (28-oz/800-g) can Italian plum tomatoes with juice

1 bay leaf

1 teaspoon sugar

2 cups (500 ml) fish or chicken stock

½ cup (125 ml) dry white wine

2 yellow potatoes, peeled and cut into ¾-inch (2-cm) chunks

18 mussels, scrubbed and debearded

18 medium shrimp, shelled and deveined

1½ pounds (675 g) firm-fleshed fish fillets (such as halibut, sea bass, or cod), cut into 2-inch (5-cm) chunks

Chopped fresh flat-leaf parsley, for garnish

(continued next page)

To make the picada, toast the almonds in a small dry skillet over medium heat, stirring frequently, until brown in spots and fragrant, about 2 minutes. Pour into a bowl to cool. Transfer the almonds and garlic to a food processor. Pulse to finely chop. Add the oil and pulse to form a thick paste. Add the parsley, pepper, and salt and pulse to blend. Transfer to a bowl and set aside.

To make the stew, heat the oil in a large, heavy pot over medium heat. Add the chorizo and brown on both sides. Using a slotted spoon, transfer to a plate lined with a paper towel.

Drain off all but 1 tablespoon fat from the pot. Add the onion and sauté over medium heat until translucent, about 3 minutes. Add the fennel, garlic, paprika, thyme, fennel seeds, and saffron. Sauté for 2 minutes. Add the tomatoes with juice, bay leaf, and sugar. Reduce the heat to medium-low and cook uncovered, stirring occasionally, until slightly thickened, 8 to 10 minutes.

Add the stock, wine, and potatoes. Bring to a boil, then reduce the heat to a simmer. Cover and cook until the potatoes are tender, about 20 minutes.

Add the mussels. Cover and cook over medium heat until all of the mussels have opened, about 5 minutes. (Discard any unopened mussels.) Add the shrimp and fish fillets to the pot, nestling them into the stock. Cover and simmer until shrimp are pink and the fish is opaque throughout, about 3 minutes.

Stir in half of the picada, then add the chorizo. Simmer gently for 2 to 3 minutes. Ladle into bowls. Remove the bay leaf. Garnish with parsley and the remaining picada.

SERVES 6

Flowering almond trees near the monastery of Santa Maria de Santes Creus, Catalonia, Spain

Almond-and-Lemon-Crusted Salmon

Roasting fresh salmon fillets with an almond and bread crumb coating infused with lemon zest creates a light and crispy crust that flavors the fish while keeping it moist and succulent. This crust also suits halibut, sole, or tilapia; adjust the cooking time accordingly.

CRUST

½ cup (2 oz/60 g) raw almonds, finely ground

½ cup (2 oz/60 g) panko (Japanese bread crumbs)

1 tablespoon minced fresh flat-leaf parsley

1 teaspoon finely grated lemon zest

½ teaspoon kosher salt

½ teaspoon freshly ground black pepper

4 (6- to 8-oz/180- to 225 g) salmon fillets, about 1 inch thick, skin and pin bones removed

1 large egg, lightly beaten

Olive oil spray

Lemon wedges, for serving

Preheat the oven to 425°F (220°C).

To make the crust, combine all the ingredients in a shallow bowl. Stir to blend.

Dip the salmon into the egg to coat both sides, shaking off the excess. Dredge in the almond bread crumbs to coat evenly on both sides. Arrange in one layer on a broiler pan. Lightly spray with olive oil. Bake until the salmon is almost cooked through but still slightly translucent in the center, 15 to 20 minutes. Serve with lemon wedges.

SERVES 4

Grilled Shrimp Skewers with Romesco Sauce

It's said that Spanish fisherman created romesco as a condiment to eat with fish in Tarragona, Catalonia. While it is indeed used as a sauce for seafood, romesco is also delicious with meat and vegetables or served as a dip or spread for bread and crudités. As with most regional specialties, myriad variations exist, but the main ingredients include a blend of dried chile, nuts, garlic, and olive oil.

ROMESCO

2 plum tomatoes, halved lengthwise

1 red bell pepper, halved lengthwise, seeded, and deveined

2 tablespoons olive oil, plus ¼ cup (60 ml)

1 large ancho chile, stemmed, seeded, and coarsely chopped

1 heaping cup ½-inch- (12-mm-) diced bread

¼ cup (1 oz/30 g) blanched almonds

3 cloves garlic, crushed

2 tablespoons red wine vinegar

1 teaspoon smoked Spanish paprika (pimentón)

1 teaspoon salt

MARINADE

¼ cup (60 ml) extra virgin olive oil

¼ cup (60 ml) fresh lemon juice

1 clove garlic, minced

1 teaspoon sweet Hungarian paprika

1 teaspoon salt

½ teaspoon ground cumin

½ teaspoon freshly ground black pepper

¼ teaspoon cayenne pepper

40 medium shrimp, about 2 pounds, (900 g) shelled, tails intact, and deveined

20 (8-inch/20-cm) bamboo skewers

To make the romesco, preheat the broiler. Arrange the tomatoes and red bell pepper, cut sides down, on a broiler pan. Broil until the skins are charred and blackened. Remove from the oven. Using tongs, put the pepper in a paper bag and let cool. Peel off and discard the skins. Coarsely chop the tomatoes and pepper and transfer to a food processor.

Heat the 2 tablespoons olive oil in a medium skillet over medium-high heat. Add the chile and sauté until it begins to turn red, 1 or 2 minutes. Using a slotted spoon, transfer to a bowl. Add the bread, almonds, and garlic to the same skillet. Sauté until golden brown, about 30 seconds. Immediately pour the mixture into the bowl with the chile.

Add the bread mixture, vinegar, paprika, and salt to a food processor. Process to combine. With the machine running, add the ¼ cup (60 ml) olive oil in a steady stream until emulsified. (The sauce should be slightly thick, like salsa. If too thick, add a little more olive oil to achieve the desired consistency.) Transfer to a small bowl. Let stand at room temperature for 1 hour to allow the flavors to develop. (Romesco may be made up to 1 day in advance. Cover and refrigerate. Bring to room temperature before serving.)

To prepare the shrimp, whisk the marinade ingredients together in a large bowl. Add the shrimp and toss to coat. Let stand for 30 minutes. Soak the bamboo skewers in water to cover while the shrimp marinate.

Prepare an outdoor grill for medium heat, or preheat the broiler. Remove the shrimp from the marinade and discard the marinade. Thread 4 shrimp side by side on two bamboo skewers to prevent shrimp from rotating when turning. Grill the shrimp over direct heat or broil 2 inches (5 cm) from the heat source, turning once, until evenly pink, 3 to 4 minutes. Transfer to a serving platter. Serve with the romesco sauce, either for dipping or spooned on top of shrimp.

MAKES 10 SKEWERS, 2 PER SERVING; SERVES 5

BAKED GOODS & DESSERTS

Almond Flour Bread

This dough yields a mild golden loaf with a subtle nutty flavor and a tight crumb due to the addition of almond flour. Use as a sandwich bread, serve thinly sliced and toasted with preserves and butter, or cube and panfry in oil for croutons.

4 cups (570 g) bread flour

1 cup (90 g) almond flour

2½ teaspoons sea salt

1 package (2¼ teaspoons) active
    dry yeast

1½ cups (375 ml) warm water
    (105° to 115°F/40° to 46°C)

3 tablespoons honey

Place the flours, sea salt, and yeast in a large bowl. Stir with a whisk to blend. Combine the warm water and honey in a small bowl. Create a well in the center of the flour and add the water, stirring until just moistened.

Turn the dough out onto a floured surface and knead until smooth and elastic, about 5 minutes. Place in a large oiled bowl, turn once to coat, and cover with a damp towel or plastic wrap. Let stand in a warm place until doubled in volume, 1½ to 2 hours. Punch the dough down and transfer to a floured surface. Divide the dough in half and form into two loaves, pinching the seams closed on the bottom. Place in two greased 4 by 8-inch (10 by 20-cm) loaf pans. Cover with a dry towel and let rise in a warm place until doubled in volume, about 45 minutes.

Preheat the oven to 425°F (220°C). Bake the bread for 15 minutes; lower the oven temperature to 375°F (190°C) and bake until golden brown and hollow sounding when tapped on the bottom, 15 to 20 minutes more.

Remove from the oven and let stand in the pans on wire racks for 5 minutes. Unmold onto the wire racks and let cool completely.

MAKES 2 (4 BY 8-INCH/10 BY 20-CM) LOAVES

Almond and Apricot Skillet Bread

Kimochdun is a festive yeast bread originating in Afghanistan and enjoyed by Muslims and Jews in Central Asia. Studded with almonds and apricots to represent wealth and good luck, the lightly sweetened bread is prepared by Muslims at the end of Ramadan. Originally kimochdun *was baked in a covered pot surrounded by coals. Today it's baked in an uncovered pot or skillet in an oven. Serve for breakfast, as a snack with tea, or as accompaniment to a plate of soft, mild cheeses.*

1 package (2¼ teaspoons) active dry yeast

¼ cup (60 ml) warm water (105° to 115°F/40° to 46°C)

2 tablespoons sugar

1¼ cups (310 ml) whole milk or goat's milk

1 tablespoon canola oil

2 teaspoons salt

3 cups (430 g) unbleached all-purpose flour, divided

1 cup (145 g) whole-wheat flour

¾ cup (115 g) unsulphured dried apricots, coarsely chopped

¾ cup (3 oz/90 g) raw almonds, coarsely chopped

Combine the yeast and water in a large mixing bowl or the bowl of a stand mixer fitted with the dough hook and stir to dissolve. Add the sugar and let stand at room temperature until foamy, about 5 minutes.
Add the milk, oil, salt, 2 cups (285 g) of the all-purpose flour, and the whole-wheat flour to the bowl. Mix to combine. Stir or mix in the remaining flour ½ cup (75 g) at a time until the dough comes together. Turn out onto a lightly floured surface and form into a ball. Place in an oiled large bowl and turn to coat. Cover with a damp towel or plastic wrap and let rise in a warm place until doubled in volume, 1½ to 2 hours.

Punch the dough down and turn out onto a floured surface. Knead for about 5 minutes, or until smooth. Cover with a dry towel and let rest for 15 minutes. Roll out the dough to a thickness of 1 inch (2.5 cm). Sprinkle with the apricots and almonds. Roll up and form the dough into a ball, pinching the bottom seams closed. Place in an oiled 9-inch (23-cm) Dutch oven or ovenproof skillet. Cover with plastic wrap or a dry towel and let rise until nearly doubled in volume, about 45 minutes.

Preheat the oven to 350°F (180°C). Slash an X in the top of the dough, running from side to side. Bake uncovered in the oven until golden brown, about 45 minutes. Unmold and let cool completely on a wire rack.

MAKES 1 (9-INCH/23-CM) ROUND LOAF

Almond and Cinnamon Kringle

Kringle means "pretzel" in Danish, and a kringle-shaped symbol is an ancient guild sign still used today by Danish bakers. Most bakeries in Denmark have a golden pretzel hanging over their entry. Inside the shops, you will find sweet and savory pretzel-shaped pastries made with puff pastry or yeast dough, sprinkled with salt and seeds or filled with nuts, raisins, almond paste or marzipan. This sweet yeast-dough kringle is a childhood favorite of the Danes, enjoyed with a cup of tea. The dough is easy to prepare, simply requiring an overnight rest before shaping and baking, so be sure to begin the recipe a day in advance. The dough can be shaped into a pretzel or a simple circular ring, as indicated below.

DOUGH

1 package (2¼ teaspoons) active
    dry yeast

¼ cup (60 ml) warm water
    (105° to 115°F/40° to 46°C)

2 cups (285 g) unbleached
    all-purpose flour

1 teaspoon ground cardamom

½ teaspoon salt

½ cup (115 g) cold unsalted butter,
    cut into cubes

2 tablespoons sugar

½ cup (125 ml) warm whole milk
    (105° to 115°F/40° to 46°C)

1 large egg, lightly beaten

FILLING

¾ cup (3 oz/90 g) sliced almonds

½ cup (145 g) almond paste

½ cup (115 g) unsalted butter,
    softened

½ cup (115 g) sugar

1 teaspoon ground cinnamon

1 teaspoon vanilla extract

TOPPING

Sugar, for coating and sprinkling

1 large egg white, lightly beaten

¼ cup (1 oz/30 g) sliced almonds

To make the dough, combine the yeast and warm water in a small bowl. Stir to dissolve the yeast, and let stand for 5 minutes, or until foamy. Combine the flour, cardamom, and salt in a large bowl and stir with a whisk to blend. Add the butter. Using your fingertips or a pastry cutter, rub or cut the butter into the flour until it resembles coarse meal. Add the yeast mixture, sugar, milk, and egg. Stir until the dough is smooth (it will be very sticky). Turn the dough out onto a floured surface and form it into a ball. Place the dough in an oiled large bowl and turn to coat. Cover with plastic wrap. Refrigerate for at least 12 or up to 24 hours.

To make the filling, combine all the ingredients in a food processor and pulse until blended.

Line a rimmed baking sheet with parchment paper. Remove the dough from the refrigerator and place on a floured surface. Knead for about 2 minutes, or until smooth. Divide the dough in half. Roll each half into a 10 by 15-inch (25 by 38-cm) rectangle. Spread half of the filling down the center of the rectangle in a 2-inch-wide (5-cm-wide) strip. Overlap the sides of the dough over the filling to make a 4-inch-wide (10-cm-wide) log. Pinch the edges to seal. Sprinkle a little sugar on a work surface and gently roll the log lengthwise to coat with the sugar. Stretch the dough around into a circle and pinch the ends together to seal in a ring. Place seam side down on the prepared baking sheet. Repeat with the remaining dough. Cover with a dry towel and let rise in a warm place until nearly double in volume, about 1 hour.

Preheat the oven to 375°F (190°C). Brush the dough with the egg white. Sprinkle with more sugar and almonds. Bake until golden, about 25 minutes. Remove from the oven, transfer from the pan to wire racks, and let cool. Serve warm or at room temperature.

MAKES 2 ROUND KRINGLES, ABOUT 8 SERVINGS EACH

Toasted Almond and Orange Biscotti with Golden Raisins

The Italian word biscotti *translates to "twice"* (bis) *"cooked"* (cotto), *and describes the method for baking these dry and crisp Roman cookies, which are perfect for dunking in coffee or dessert wine. Biscotti usually include almonds, but many variations with chocolate and dried fruit abound. This version uses golden raisins and orange zest, resulting in a sweet and festive cookie.*

A Dessert, Raphaelle Peale, 1814

¾ cup (180 g) sugar

½ cup (115 g) unsalted butter, softened

1 large egg

1 tablespoon finely grated orange zest

1 teaspoon vanilla extract

½ teaspoon ground cinnamon

2¼ cups (330 g) unbleached all-purpose flour

1 teaspoon baking powder

½ teaspoon baking soda

½ teaspoon salt

¾ cup (3 oz/90 g) raw almonds, toasted (see page 41) and chopped

½ cup (90 g) golden raisins

Preheat the oven to 350°F (180°C). Line a baking sheet with parchment paper.

Cream the sugar and butter together on medium-high speed in a stand mixer fitted with the paddle attachment. Add the egg, zest, vanilla, and cinnamon and mix to combine on medium speed. Combine the flour, baking powder, baking soda, and salt in a medium bowl. Stir with a whisk to combine. Add to the egg mixture and mix on medium-low speed until combined. Stir in the almonds and raisins.

Divide the dough in half. Form each into a log and flatten to a width of 2 inches (5 cm). Arrange each log on the prepared baking sheet. Bake until light golden and set, about 30 minutes. Remove from the oven and let cool for 20 minutes.

Using a serrated knife, cut into slices ¾-inch (2-cm) thick. Arrange the slices, cut side down, on the same baking sheet. Return to the oven and bake until golden brown, about 15 minutes. Remove and let cool completely on the racks. Biscotti may be stored in an airtight container for up to 4 days.

MAKES 24 BISCOTTI

Salted Almond Butter Cookies with Chocolate Chunks

Fresh, creamy butter flecked with fleur de sel is a luxurious European tradition, often enjoyed slathered on a fresh baguette. Sea salt loves sugar, balancing sweetness and prodding us to have more In this recipe, flakes of fleur de sel are whipped into the cookie batter, where they remain intact, complementing the golden flavor of the almond butter and studding the dough with tiny, crunchy bursts of salt.

1¾ cups (255 g) unbleached all-purpose flour

2 teaspoons baking soda

½ teaspoon salt

1 cup (225 g) unsalted butter, softened

1 cup (220 g) firmly packed dark brown sugar

¾ cup (180 g) granulated sugar

1 large egg

1 teaspoon vanilla extract

1 cup (225 g) unsalted creamy almond butter (see page 54)

1 teaspoon fleur de sel or flaky sea salt, plus extra for sprinkling

8 ounces (225 g) dark chocolate (70 to 72 percent), coarsely chopped

Combine the flour, baking soda, and salt in a medium bowl and stir with a whisk to blend. Cream the butter and sugars together in a stand mixer fitted with the paddle attachment on medium-high speed until light and fluffy. Scrape down the sides and bottom of the bowl. Beat in the egg and vanilla.

Add the almond butter and the 1 teaspoon fleur de sel and mix until smooth. Stir in the flour mixture until just combined. Fold in the chocolate. Cover the bowl with plastic wrap and refrigerate for at least 1 hour or up to 24 hours.

Preheat the oven to 375°F (190°C). Line a baking sheet with parchment paper. Drop the dough onto the baking sheet by rounded tablespoons 2 inches (5 cm) apart. Sprinkle with a few grains of fleur de sel. Bake until lightly golden brown, about 12 minutes. Remove from the oven and transfer the parchment, with cookies, to a wire rack to cool.

MAKES 36 TO 40 (2-INCH/5-CM) COOKIES

Almond Florentines

Florentines are classic Christmas cookies with a mysterious provenance. Their name implies an Italian origin, while their method is decidedly French, but there is little question that Florentines are a delicious treat. Toasted almonds, orange, and caramel weave together to form a lacy cookie that is drizzled with dark chocolate. No wonder both countries are happy to call this recipe their own.

1¼ cups (5 oz/145 g) sliced almonds, lightly toasted (see page 41)

¼ cup (45 g) unbleached all-purpose flour

Finely grated zest of 1 orange, about 1 tablespoon

½ teaspoon sea salt

½ cup (115 g) granulated sugar

¼ cup (60 g) firmly packed light brown sugar

¼ cup (60 ml) heavy cream

4 tablespoons (60 g) unsalted butter

3½ ounces (105 g) dark chocolate, chopped

Preheat the oven to 350°F (180°C). Line a baking sheet with parchment paper.

Coarsely chop ¾ cup (90 g) of the almonds. Place in a medium bowl. Add the remaining almonds, flour, orange zest, and salt. Mix with a fork to combine.

Place the sugars, cream, and butter in a medium saucepan. Cook over medium heat, stirring constantly, until the sugar dissolves and the butter melts. Increase the heat to high. Bring to a boil, then remove from the heat and pour over the almonds. Stir to thoroughly combine.

Drop spoonfuls of batter 3 inches (7.5 cm) apart onto the prepared baking sheet (they will spread as they bake). Bake one baking sheet at a time, rotating the pan once or twice to ensure even cooking, for 10 to 12 minutes, or until the cookies are golden brown. Remove from the oven and let cool on the pan on a wire rack for 5 minutes. Using a thin spatula, transfer the cookies to wire racks to let cool completely.

Melt the chocolate in a double boiler over barely simmering water, stirring occasionally until smooth. Dip a fork in the chocolate and drizzle the chocolate over the cookies. Allow the chocolate to set before serving.

MAKES ABOUT 20 (4-INCH/10-CM) COOKIES

Pear and Almond Frangipane Tart

If you've enjoyed French or Italian desserts, chances are you've tasted frangipane, an almond pastry cream that's used as a filling for tarts, cakes, and pastries. In this rustic and aromatic tart, frangipane forms a rich base for pears. The dough is pressed into the tart pan without rolling, resulting in a cookie-like shell. For best results, choose Anjou or Bosc pears, which hold their shape while baking. The tart may be prepared up to a day in advance but is best on the day of preparation. Serve with whipped cream.

PASTRY SHELL

1½ cups (225 g) unbleached
    all-purpose flour

½ cup (115 g) sugar

½ teaspoon salt

½ cup (115 g) cold unsalted butter,
    cut into ½-inch (12-mm) cubes

1 large egg yolk

2 to 3 tablespoons ice water

FILLING

4 to 5 ripe but firm Anjou or
    Bosc pears

Juice of ½ lemon

⅔ cup (145 g) sugar

½ cup (115 g) unsalted butter,
    softened

1 large egg

1 large egg yolk

⅞ cup (3½ oz/105 g) raw almonds,
    finely ground

2 tablespoons all-purpose flour

2 tablespoons pear brandy

1 teaspoon vanilla extract

½ teaspoon almond extract

GLAZE

½ cup (145 g) apricot preserves

1 tablespoon water

(continued next page)

ALMOND EXTRACT EXTRAS

Almond extract is an essential ingredient in the baker's kitchen. A scant teaspoon will enhance desserts and baked goods with the subtle hint of sweet almond. When used generously, it will tip a dessert into a bold almond confection.

Not all almond extracts are alike. In pure almond extract, the almond flavor is created by benzaldehyde, a natural substance extracted from the kernels of bitter almonds and stone fruit, while in imitation almond extract, the flavor is derived from synthetic benzaldehyde. In either form, the almond flavor is amplified by alcohol. The amount of alcohol varies by brand; the more alcohol, the stronger the flavor. Whether you opt for pure or imitation almond extract, one bottle will go a long way. Here are a few suggestions on how to put it to good use.

• *Where there is cream*: Try adding a few drops of almond extract to flavor whipped cream, homemade ice creams, gelatos, and custards.

• *Almonds love fruit*: Add almond extract to fruit-based cakes, tarts, compotes, and crisps.

• *Heat it up*: Flavor warm beverages with a few drops of almond, including coffee drinks, warm milk, chai, and hot chocolate.

• *Good to the grain*: Almonds are a great match with grains. Add almond extract to rice puddings, oatmeal, and granola.

• *Give vanilla a rest*: Substitute almond extract for vanilla in baked goods such as cakes, cookies, meringues, and muffins.

To make the pastry shell, butter a 9-inch (23-cm) tart pan. Combine the flour, sugar, and salt in a food processor. Pulse to combine. Add the butter and pulse until the dough resembles coarse meal. Add the egg yolk and pulse just until moist clumps form. Transfer the dough to a bowl. Add 2 tablespoons water and mix with a fork until the dough begins to stick together. If necessary, add 1 more tablespoon water. Turn the dough into the tart pan. Gently press evenly over the bottom and up the sides without overworking the dough. Refrigerate for 1 hour.

Preheat the oven to 375°F (190°C). Butter a piece of aluminum foil and press, buttered side down, into the tart shell, making sure you fit it into the sides. Bake until lightly browned, about 25 minutes.

Still Life of Grapes, Nuts, Miniature Pears and a Bee, Giovanna Garzoni, c.1630

To make the filling, peel and halve the pears lengthwise. Scoop out the core and cut out the stem with a paring knife. Thinly slice each pear half crosswise, keeping the halves intact. Lightly sprinkle with lemon juice; set aside. Cream the sugar and butter together in a large bowl until light and fluffy. Beat in the egg and egg yolk. Stir in the almonds, flour, brandy, vanilla, and almond extract until just combined. Do not overmix. Spread the filling in the bottom of the prebaked pastry shell. Arrange each pear half over the filling in a spoke pattern, beginning in the center with the narrow end of each pear, slightly fanning out the slices and gently pressing them into the filling. Bake until the filling is firm and golden, 45 minutes to 1 hour. (If the crust browns before the center is set, place a foil collar around the rim of the crust to prevent burning). Remove the tart from the oven and transfer to a wire rack to cool in the pan.

While the tart is baking, make the glaze: Heat the preserves and water in a small saucepan over medium heat, stirring once or twice, until liquefied. Strain through a fine-mesh sieve.

Brush the warm tart with the glaze. As the tart cools, the glaze will set. To serve, remove the sides of the pan, cut the tart into wedges, and serve slightly warm or at room temperature with whipped cream if desired.

MAKES 1 (9-INCH/23-CM) TART; SERVES 8 TO 10

Lemon Semolina and Almond Cake with Olive Oil and Honey

Namoura *is the Lebanese name for this luscious cake, which combines the Middle Eastern flavors of honey, olive oil, and lemon with a crowning touch of almonds. The dry baked cake will soak up the syrup like a sponge, resulting in a moist and sticky treat to serve with tea.*

¾ cup (180 g) sugar

¾ cup (175 ml) extra virgin olive oil

½ cup (125 ml) whole milk

4 large eggs

2 teaspoons finely grated lemon zest

1½ cups (225 g) semolina flour

½ cup (60 g) almond flour

2 teaspoons baking powder

1 teaspoon baking soda

¾ teaspoon kosher salt

SYRUP

½ cup (115 g) sugar

⅓ cup (75 ml) fresh lemon juice

¼ cup (90 g) honey

Sliced almonds, for decorating

Preheat the oven to 350°F (180°C). Oil an 8-inch (20-cm) square baking pan. Line the bottom with parchment paper and oil the paper.

Whisk the sugar, olive oil, and milk together in a large bowl. Add the eggs and lemon zest and whisk to combine. Combine the flours, baking powder, baking soda, and salt together in a medium bowl. Stir with a whisk to blend. Add to the wet ingredients and whisk until smooth. Pour into the prepared pan. (The batter will be very thin).

Bake in the oven until the top is set and golden and a skewer inserted in the center comes out clean, about 50 minutes. Remove from the oven and let cool slightly in the pan on a wire rack.

While the cake is baking, prepare the syrup. Combine all the syrup ingredients in a small saucepan. Cook over medium heat, whisking to dissolve the sugar. When the syrup comes to a boil, remove from the heat.

While the cake is still warm, cut into 2-inch (5-cm) squares without removing from the pan. Pour the syrup over the cake. Scatter the sliced almonds over the cake. Let cool completely to allow the flavors to develop. Store in an airtight container for up to 3 days.

MAKES 1 (8-INCH/20-CM) CAKE; SERVES 16

Chocolate-Amaretto Torte

Torta caprese is a flourless chocolate and almond cake from the Italian island of Capri. The story goes that a local baker forgot to add flour to his batter—with divine results. This recipe amends the original torta caprese by adding a little flour to bind the batter, while fortifying the cake with amaretto-soaked raisins. The finished cake is coated with a dark chocolate glaze and showered with sliced and chopped nuts, producing a rich dessert redolent of almonds.

½ cup (90 g) golden raisins

⅓ cup (75 ml) amaretto liqueur

2 tablespoons unsweetened cocoa powder

14 ounces (420 g) dark chocolate (70 to 72 percent), chopped

1 cup (225 g) unsalted butter

6 large eggs, separated

1 cup (225 g) sugar

⅞ cup (3½ oz/105 g) raw almonds, toasted (see page 41) and finely ground

½ cup (75 g) unbleached all-purpose flour

1 teaspoon vanilla extract

1 teaspoon almond extract

½ teaspoon salt

GLAZE

8 ounces (225 g) dark chocolate (70 to 72 percent), chopped

½ cup (115 g) unsalted butter

½ teaspoon almond extract

⅞ cup (3½ oz/105 g) raw almonds, toasted (see page 41) and finely chopped, for garnish

¼ cup (1 oz/30 g) sliced almonds for garnish

(continued next page)

Combine the raisins and amaretto in a small bowl. Let stand at room temperature for at least 30 minutes.

Preheat the oven to 350°F (180°C). Butter a 10-inch (25-cm) springform pan. Line the bottom with a round of parchment paper and butter the parchment. Coat the bottom and sides with cocoa, tapping out the excess.

Melt the chocolate and butter in a double boiler over barely simmering water, stirring until smooth.

Beat the egg yolks and sugar with an electric mixer on medium-high speed until light in color and thickened, about 3 minutes. Add the chocolate mixture, raisins with amaretto, almonds, flour, vanilla, almond extract, and salt. Stir to combine.

Beat the egg whites in a clean bowl of an electric mixer until they form stiff, glossy peaks. Stir one-fourth of the beaten whites into the chocolate. Gently fold in the remaining egg whites until blended.

Pour into the prepared cake pan. Bake until the top of the cake is just set (it will still be moist in the center), 40 to 45 minutes. Remove from the oven and let cool completely on a wire rack.

While the cake is cooling, prepare the glaze. Melt the chocolate and butter in a double boiler over barely simmering water, stirring until smooth. Stir in the almond extract.

Invert the cake on a plate and remove the sides and bottom of the pan along with the parchment paper. Pour the glaze over the cake, smoothing it with an offset icing spatula. Toss the finely chopped almonds onto the sides of the cake. Top the cake with the sliced almonds. Refrigerate for at least 2 hours or overnight.

MAKES 1 (10-INCH/25-CM) CAKE; SERVES 10 TO 12

Almond-Fig Tea Cakes

Brown butter adds an extra-nutty richness to these luscious tea cakes fragrant with almond. If fresh figs are not available, dried figs may be substituted. Alternatively, top each cake with 1 or 2 fresh raspberries in place of a fig slice.

Aaron with Blossoming Almond Rod Before the Ark of the Covenant, c.1360

¾ cup (180 g) unsalted butter

1½ cups (180 g) confectioners' sugar, sifted, plus extra for dusting

¾ cup (60 g) almond flour

½ cup (75 g) unbleached all-purpose flour

¼ teaspoon salt

5 large egg whites

1½ teaspoons almond extract

8 small ripe figs, stemmed and sliced crosswise in thirds, or 12 small dried figs, halved lengthwise

Preheat the oven to 375°F (190°C). Melt the butter in a small saucepan over medium-low heat until fragrant and lightly browned, about 5 minutes. (Watch it carefully, because it can quickly change from brown to burnt.) Strain through a fine-mesh sieve into a heatproof bowl. Let cool slightly. Pour the clear browned butter into a small pitcher and discard the brown solids on the bottom of the bowl.

Combine the 1½ cups (180 g) sugar, the almond flour, all-purpose flour, and salt in the bowl of a stand mixer fitted with the whisk attachment. Mix to blend. Add the egg whites and mix until just combined. Add the browned butter and the almond extract. Mix until very smooth. Use now, or cover and refrigerate for up to 3 days.

Butter 24 mini muffin cups. Divide the batter evenly among the cups and top each with a fig slice. Bake until golden brown and just cooked through, 15 to 18 minutes. Let cool in pan on a wire rack for 10 minutes. Unmold onto wire racks and let cool completely. Serve dusted with confectioners' sugar.

MAKES 24 (1¹/₂-INCH/4-CM) TEA CAKES

Almond Semifreddo and Port Wine–Poached Figs with Almond Praline

Semifreddo, *which means "half-frozen," is a light and airy Italian cream dessert that does not require an ice cream machine to make. Almonds and orange zest fleck this semifreddo, which is drizzled with a richly spiced fig compote and topped with shards of praline. If you can't find fresh figs, dried figs may be substituted. The semifreddo should be served within 24 hours.*

SEMIFREDDO

⅔ cup (2½ oz/75 g) raw almonds, toasted (see page 41)

½ cup (115 g) sugar, divided

½ teaspoon finely grated orange zest

¼ teaspoon sea salt

3 large egg whites, at room temperature★

1 cup (250 ml) cold heavy cream

½ teaspoon almond extract, or 2 teaspoons amaretto liqueur

¼ teaspoon vanilla extract

FIGS

1 cup (250 ml) port or red wine

½ cup (125 ml) balsamic vinegar

¼ cup (60 ml) fresh orange juice

2 tablespoons honey

1 cinnamon stick

2 whole cloves

½ teaspoon black peppercorns

16 medium-ripe fresh figs or large, plump dried figs, stemmed and halved lengthwise

PRALINE

½ cup (115 g) sugar

½ cup (2 oz/60 g) sliced almonds, lightly toasted (see page 41)

½ teaspoon salt

★*Note: This recipe contains raw eggs.*

(continued next page)

To make the semifreddo, line a 9 by 5-inch (23 by 13-cm) loaf pan with plastic wrap, leaving a 3-inch (7.5-cm) overhang on all sides.

Place the almonds and ¼ cup (60 g) of the sugar in a food processor. Pulse until finely ground. Add the orange zest and salt; pulse to blend.

Beat the egg whites with an electric mixer on high speed until they begin to hold soft peaks. Add the remaining ¼ cup (60 g) sugar, 1 tablespoon at a time, and beat until stiff, glossy peaks form.

In a deep bowl, beat the cream and almond and vanilla extracts on high speed until soft peaks form. Gently fold the beaten whites into the cream until blended. Gently fold the almonds into the cream mixture until evenly distributed. Spoon into the prepared baking dish and smooth the top. Cover with plastic and freeze for at least 8 hours or overnight.

To prepare the figs, combine all of the ingredients except the figs in a heavy medium saucepan and bring to a boil over medium-high heat. Cook until the liquid is reduced by two-thirds and syrupy in consistency, 10 to 12 minutes. Strain through a fine-mesh sieve and return to the pan. Add the figs and gently stir to coat. If using fresh figs, simmer for 5 minutes over medium-low heat, stirring occasionally. If using dried figs, simmer until softened, about 10 minutes. Remove from the heat and let cool completely.

To make the praline, line a baking sheet with parchment paper. Heat the sugar in a small, heavy saucepan over medium heat until it melts, stirring occasionally with a wooden spoon. Continue to cook, stirring constantly, until the sugar turns amber in color. Add the almonds and salt and stir quickly to coat. Pour onto the prepared baking sheet and spread into a thin layer with a wet spatula. Do not touch with your fingers. Let cool completely. Break into 1½-inch (4-cm) pieces.

To assemble the dessert, grasp the sides of the plastic liner and gently lift the semifreddo from the loaf pan onto a cutting board. Carefully slide the liner out from under the semifreddo and discard. Cut the loaf into ¾-inch (2-cm) slices and place a slice in each of 8 to 10 shallow soup bowls. Spoon the figs and syrup over the semifreddo. Garnish with praline pieces and serve immediately.

SERVES 8 TO 10

Moroccan Rice Pudding

Rice pudding is a standard dessert in many European and Middle Eastern cultures. This recipe takes inspiration from the Moroccan roz bil halib, *with the addition of raisins and honey. Typically, the rice is first boiled in water, then simmered in milk. In this version, almond milk is substituted for the water. Orange flower water, which may be purchased in Middle Eastern markets or the international section of your supermarket, replaces the traditional rose water in this variation. Cointreau, or another orange-flavored liqueur, may be substituted for the flower water for a spirited version.*

½ cup (90 g) raisins

2 tablespoons orange flower water

1¼ cups (310 ml) unsweetened
   almond milk (see page 56)

2 tablespoons sugar

1 cup (210 g) Arborio rice

4½ cups (1.1l) whole milk

2 tablespoons unsalted butter

1 (3-inch/7.5-cm) cinnamon stick

1 teaspoon almond extract

½ teaspoon salt

⅓ cup (1½ oz/45 g) raw almonds,
   toasted (see page 41) and
   coarsely chopped

Honey, for drizzling

Combine the raisins and orange flower water in a small bowl. Set aside.

Heat the almond milk and sugar in a large pot, stirring to dissolve the sugar. Add the rice. Bring to a boil, then reduce the heat to low. Cover and simmer until most of the liquid is absorbed.

Add 3 cups (750 ml) of the whole milk, the butter, cinnamon stick, almond extract, and salt to the rice. Simmer over medium-low heat, stirring frequently to prevent sticking, until the rice is thickened. Add the remaining milk, ½ cup (125 ml) at a time, stirring until the milk is absorbed before adding more milk each time. The rice pudding should be thickened but not stiff. The cooking process will take approximately 45 minutes. Remove from the heat and discard the cinnamon stick.

Spoon the pudding into 4 bowls. Sprinkle with the raisins and almonds and drizzle with a little honey. Serve warm or chilled.

SERVES 4

AMARETTO AND AMARETTI

What do you get when you cross almonds with a Renaissance painter and a beautiful Italian widow? A portrait of the woman— forever immortalized as the face of the Madonna, in a fresco for the chapel of Santa Maria dei Miracoli in Saronno (now in the Louvre)—and the liqueur, amaretto di Saronno, that legend says the widow created for the artist.

Amaretto is an almond-flavored liqueur made with almonds or apricot pits. *Amaretto* is the diminutive of the Italian word for bitter, *amaro*, a reference to the pleasing aroma associated with bitter almonds. Both whipped cream and tiramisù, the dessert of sponge cake soaked with spirits and espresso and layered with a filling of mascarpone cheese, are sometimes flavored with amaretto. The liqueur is served with or without ice and is an ingredient in many cocktails.

Amaretto cookies, or amaretti, are crisp on the outside and soft on the inside. Some desserts, notably sweets with peaches or other relatives of the almond, call for amaretti crumbled on top.

Plum Trifle with Amaretti

Sumptuous trifles are a British tradition: billowy parfaits of fruit and cream layered with sponge cake, ladyfingers, or cookies. This trifle layers crisp amaretti cookies, the Italian version of almond macaroons, with an almond-infused plum compote and ripples of custard cream. Store-bought amaretti may be substituted for homemade.

Adoration of the Magi, Bernardino Luini, c.1525

AMARETTI

1 cup (225 g) granulated sugar

8 ounces (225 g) almond paste

3 large egg whites

Pearl sugar (optional)

COMPOTE

2 pounds (900 g) plums, halved
    and pitted

½ cup (115 g) granulated sugar

1 teaspoon almond extract

½ teaspoon ground cinnamon

CUSTARD CREAM AND TOPPING

2 large egg yolks

4 tablespoons (60 g) granulated sugar

½ vanilla bean, split lengthwise

½ cup (125 ml) whole milk

1½ cups (375 ml) heavy cream

1 tablespoon amaretto liqueur

To make the amaretti, preheat the oven to 350°F (180°C). Line two baking sheets with parchment paper.

Process the sugar in a food processor until superfine. Add the almond paste and process until finely crumbled. Add the egg whites, one at a time, pulsing after each addition, then process until smooth.

With either a pastry bag or a spoon, pipe or drop 1-inch (2.5-cm) mounds of batter onto the prepared baking sheets. Sprinkle with pearl sugar, if using. Bake until lightly golden and cracked, 12 to 15 minutes. Remove from the oven and let cool completely on wire racks. (Makes about 3 dozen cookies.)

(continued next page)

To make the compote, cut each plum half into ½-inch-thick (12-mm-thick) slices. Place in a large saucepan with the sugar, almond extract, and cinnamon.

Cook over medium heat, stirring, until the sugar dissolves. Reduce the heat to medium-low. Cook, stirring occasionally, until the plums are soft and syrupy, about 10 minutes. Remove from the heat and let cool completely.

To make the custard cream, whisk the egg yolks and 2 tablespoons of the sugar together in a medium saucepan. In another medium saucepan, scrape the vanilla seeds into the milk and add the pods to the pan. Cook over medium-low heat until bubbles form around the edges of the pan. Stir 2 tablespoons of the milk into the eggs. Slowly add the remaining milk, stirring constantly. Heat the milk mixture over medium heat, stirring constantly with a wooden spoon, until the custard thickens to the consistency of heavy cream and coats the wooden spoon, about 4 minutes. Do not let the custard boil. Remove from the heat and strain through a fine-meshed sieve into a bowl. Set aside and let cool completely.

Beat the heavy cream on high speed with an electric mixer until traces of the beaters are visible in the cream. Add the remaining 2 tablespoons sugar and the amaretto. Beat until soft peaks form. Gently fold half of the whipped cream into the custard.

To assemble the trifle, spoon a thin layer of the compote into the bottom of a large glass serving bowl or 8 individual glass goblets. Crumble a layer of amaretti over the compote. Cover with half of the custard cream. Top with half of the remaining compote. Crumble another layer of amaretti over the compote. Cover with the remaining custard cream. Top with the remaining compote. Crumble a final layer of amaretti over the compote. Spoon the reserved whipped cream over the top of the trifle. Dot the top of the trifle with crumbled amaretti.

Serve immediately, or refrigerate for up to 4 hours. The longer the trifle sits, the softer it will become.

SERVES 8

Chocolate Almond Bark with Raisins and Chile

This easy, no-bake dessert is perfect for the holidays. Studded with almonds and raisins and spiced with an Aztec blend of chili powder, cinnamon, and cayenne, it will liven up any dessert table or gift basket. The balance of heat, spice, and salt is addictive, so consider making a double batch. Choose the best quality of chocolate you can find.

12 ounces (350 g) dark chocolate (70 to 72 percent), chopped

¾ teaspoon ancho chile powder

½ teaspoon ground cinnamon

¼ teaspoon cayenne pepper, or to taste

1 cup (4 oz/115 g) raw almonds, toasted (see page 41) and coarsely chopped

¾ cup (115 g) raisins

Sea salt (optional)

Line a baking sheet with parchment paper.

Melt two-thirds (8 oz/225 g) of the chocolate in the bowl of a double boiler, stirring frequently until smooth. Remove from the heat and add the remaining chocolate. Stir until all the chocolate is melted and smooth. Stir in the chile powder, cinnamon, and cayenne. Add half of the almonds and half of the raisins to the chocolate.

Pour the chocolate onto the baking sheet, smoothing it out in a thin, even layer with a spatula. Sprinkle with the remaining nuts and raisins, gently pressing them into the chocolate. Sprinkle with sea salt, if using.

Refrigerate until firm, about 30 minutes. Break into 1½-inch (4-cm) pieces to serve. Store in an airtight container in the refrigerator for up to 2 weeks.

MAKES ABOUT 1 POUND (450 g)

Almond Granita with Raspberries

As if we needed another reason to love Italy, breakfasts there often include a sweet cookie, cake, or frozen granita. In Sicily, almond granita is served for breakfast in a brioche. We call this recipe "dessert" and omit the brioche, while adding raspberries in syrup for a sweet treat. Be sure that the raspberry syrup is well chilled before serving; otherwise it will melt the granita.

GRANITA

3 cups (750 ml) unsweetened almond milk (see page 56)

⅓ cup (90 g) sugar

¼ cup (75 g) almond paste

¼ teaspoon almond extract, or to taste

RASPBERRIES IN SYRUP

⅓ cup (90 g) sugar

⅓ cup (75 ml) water

½ teaspoon ground cardamom

2 cups (225 g) fresh raspberries

¼ cup (1 oz/30 g) sliced almonds, toasted (see page 41)

To make the granita, process the almond milk, sugar, almond paste, and almond extract in a blender or food processor until smooth. Strain through a fine-mesh sieve into an 8-inch (20-cm) square metal baking pan. Freeze for 1 hour. Stir with a fork, breaking apart any frozen clumps, and freeze again for 2 hours. Scrape with a fork to break into flakes. Serve immediately, or freeze for up to 3 days. Before serving, scrape with a fork.

To make the berries in syrup, combine the sugar, water, and cardamom in a small saucepan. Bring to a boil over medium-high heat, stirring until the sugar is dissolved. Remove from the heat and stir in the raspberries. Let cool completely. The syrup may be prepared up to 6 hours in advance. Cover and refrigerate until use.

To serve, divide the granita among 6 bowls. Spoon some of the raspberries and a little syrup over the granita. Garnish with sliced almonds.

SERVES 6

ALMONDS IN SICILY

Traveling through Sicily in February, you are rewarded by the profusion of the white-pink flowers of one of the major crops of the island. Almonds have thrived in Sicily since the third century BCE. Three varieties have become part of Sicilian culture: the hard-shelled sweet *sativa*, the bitter *amara*, and the soft-shelled *fragilis*. Rarely exported, these precious fruits are used extensively in classic Sicilian sweet and savory dishes.

One well-known foodstuff was introduced into Sicilian cuisine by the Arabs in the ninth century: almond-sugar paste, or marzipan, which is used to create a shell-like topping for cake (*cassata Siciliana*) and shaped into various fruits and vegetables and painted with vegetable dyes to make a confection known as *frutta di Martorana*. Almond milk is served as a refreshing drink and used as a base for almond gelato, while many different kinds of cookies, including amaretti, are made with sweet almonds.

—PAMELA SHELDON JOHNS, cooking instructor and author of *Sicily (Silver Spoon Kitchen)*, and *Cucina Povera: Tuscan Peasant Cooking*

Acknowledgments

It became clear, after our first glorious day visiting an almond farm and processing plant, that we had to make a book about almonds. Everything about almonds captivated us—their storied history; their complete reliance on bees for pollination; their fuzzy green hulls, soft in spring, but tough and weathered in fall.

What wasn't so clear was whether other people would feel the same way. We found out quickly that we were not alone. Nearly every single person we have encountered—both strangers and long-time friends and family—had a universal reaction. "Almonds? You mean the nut?" When we answered, "Yes, the nut," their immediate reply was, "I love almonds! I eat them every day!" There then came a steady litany of the daily habits of almond consumers. We repeatedly heard: "I eat seven to ten a day." "I have almond milk with my cereal." "I have almond milk in my smoothie." "I have almond butter on my toast!" Almond lovers were everywhere.

We are indebted to many people for creating this book. A bouquet of thanks and blossoming almond branches goes to Jenny Barry, our project manager and extraordinary designer, muse, editor, and friend. Her wisdom and steady pace kept us pointing true north.

Bob Holmes shared his gifts with us once again, capturing in his photos the sublime in nature and in food. These pages sing with his expert eye. For their help with the food photography, special thanks go to assistant photographer Andrea Johnson, food stylist Kim Kissling, and prop stylist Carol Hacker.

Lynda Balslev's recipes are the heart of this book; her ability to transform many of them from near and far into almond-centered ones—adding flavors, history, and cooking tips—will entice even the most timid of cooks into the kitchen.

We're indebted to well-known chefs and food writers who contributed sidebars and made this book international: special thanks to Maureen Abood, Michael Anthony, Lynda Balslev, Georgeanne Brennan, Terrence Brennan, Gerard Craft, Janet Fletcher, Cheryl Forberg, Joyce Goldstein, Blake Hallanan, Pamela Sheldon Johns, Farina Wong Kingsley, Susana Trilling, and Suneeta Vaswani.

Janice Fuhrman helped shape the manuscript and deserves many thanks for meeting an impossible deadline. Carolyn Miller's copyediting made everyone's writing shine, and Madeleine Fentress offered helpful suggestions as well. We also thank Christina Bryant, Clare Fentress, and Sam Fentress for their help with the manuscript and for being thoughtful readers.

We're equally grateful to Gibbs Smith and our editor, Madge Baird, who recognized that this cookbook had wide appeal.

The almond industry is full of special people, and we owe many of them deep thanks. To Ryon Paton and Bill Hooper at Trinitas Farms: thanks for driving us through the dusty back roads of Manteca and showing us amazing vistas of almond orchards. Scott Phippen, thank you for sharing a day with us and teaching us, from a farmer's perspective, about almonds.

Bob Wilhelm has been invaluable; his long-standing place in agricultural marketing allowed us to meet many talented people in Manteca and Sacramento, including Brandon Souza and Ross Harvey. At Blue Diamond Growers, we are grateful to Cassandra Keyse, and at the Almond Board of California we have many people to thank for their support and for eagerly sharing research and information: Richard Waycott, Dave Phippen, Melissa Mautz, Jenny Konshak, and Jenny Heap.

We had expert advice that we want to acknowledge: thank you George Seay, Peb Jackson, Craig Wenning, Rich Stim, Eric Kittner, Ken Harrington, Jack Taylor, Ken Olsen, Stephen Koenig, and Elizabeth Wyckoff.

For steady friendship and encouragement, thank you to Derek and Justin Bryant; Paul, Jane, Sam, and Joseph Fentress; Anna Monticelli; Mary Chapman Webster; Marylen Mann; Lisa Queen; Joan DeMayo; Annie Presley Selanders, Christie Murphy; Polly Pollack. Most of all, thank you to our families, who provided daily sustenance of the best kind—their enduring love.

—Barbara Bryant and Betsy Fentress

Additional Image Credits

Index

Further Reading

We are most grateful to the Almond Board of California for providing facts, statistics, and general information about almonds for this cookbook. More information is available on their vastly resourceful website: www.almonds.com

Agnew, Singeli. "The Almond and the Bee." *SF Gate Magazine*, October 2007.

Allen, Gray. *The Almond People: Blue Diamond Growers at 90: a history of Blue Diamond Growers upon the celebration of 90 years of service and leadership in California's almond industry*. Sacramento, California: Blue Diamond Growers, 2000.

McGee, Harold. *On Food and Cooking: The Science and Lore of the Kitchen*. New York: Scribner, 2004.

McKibben, Bill. "Of Mites and Men." *Orion Magazine*, July/August 2006.

McNamee, Gregory. *Moveable Feasts: The History, Science, and Lore of Food*. Lincoln, Nebraska: Bison Books, 2008.

Micke, Warren C., ed. *Almond Production Manual*. Davis, California: University of California Agriculture and Natural Resources Publications, 1996.

Oliver, Randy. "2012 Almond Pollination Update." *American Bee Journal*, April 2012.

Vehling, Joseph Dommers, ed. and trans. *Apicius: Cookery and Dining in Ancient Rome*. Mineola, New York: Dover Publications, 1977.

2012 Almond Almanac. Modesto, California: Almond Board of California.

The website of Jordan Almonds: www.jordanalmonds.com